CONVERSATIONS WITH ROGER SESSIONS

CONVERSATIONS WITH

ROGER

SESSIONS

Andrea Olmstead

NORTHEASTERN UNIVERSITY PRESS
BOSTON

Northeastern University Press

Copyright © 1987 by Andrea Olmstead

The first few bars of *Montezuma* (page 132) are used by permission of the publisher. For complete works by Roger Sessions, please contact Hal Leonard Publishing Corp., 8112 West Bluemound Road, Milwaukee, Wisconsin 53213.

Library of Congress Cataloging in Publication Data

Sessions, Roger, 1896–1985.
   Conversations with Roger Sessions.
   "List of works and recordings": p.
   Bibliography: p.
   Includes index.
   1. Sessions, Roger, 1896–1985.   2. Composers— United States—Interviews.   I. Olmstead, Andrea. II. Title.
ML410.S473A5   1987   780'.92'4   86-31290
ISBN 1-55553-010-9

Designed by Daniel Earl Thaxton.

Composed in Perpetua by Graphic Composition, Athens, Georgia.
Printed and bound by Murray Printing Company, Westford, Massachusetts. The paper is Glatfelter Offset, an acid-free sheet.

MANUFACTURED IN THE UNITED STATES OF AMERICA
91   90   89   88   87   5   4   3   2   1

To Larry Bell

CONTENTS

ILLUSTRATIONS

INTRODUCTION

The first work of Roger Sessions I heard was the premiere of his Concerto for Violin and Violoncello in November of 1971 at the Juilliard School in New York. After the performance the violinist next to me commented, "Oh, it's just another twelve-tone piece." I did not understand the remark because, as a violinist myself, I simply did not relate that feature to the beauty and virtuosity of the piece. Sessions rose to take a bow and struck me as formidable and remote.

The following summer Sessions was a composer in residence at the Aspen Music Festival in Colorado. There the Double Concerto was repeated and his 1972 Concertino for Orchestra was also played. Both these works were his newest to date, and the composer was still excited about them, as evidenced by his decidedly un-seventy-five-year-old sprint down the aisle of the tent to congratulate the conductor. This young-acting man had been known for the past fifty years as one of the two most famous American composers—the other was Aaron Copland. Sessions's contributions to musical life had included numerous orchestral works, two operas, and many other works, as well as four books, and decades of teaching. His name had been paired with Copland's since 1928, when Copland presented a series of Copland–Sessions concerts in New York and Europe. But like many such musical pairs, there were more differences between the two than similarities. Sessions was not interested in Americanism for its own sake and wrote what might be called abstract music. Both gained considerable recognition—Copland by a larger public, and Sessions within the realm of composers and musicians.

It turned out that Roger Sessions shared an office, Room 516, with the music history faculty at Juilliard, which I joined in 1972. Not wishing to intrude on his private lessons, I avoided the office on Tuesdays and Wednesdays. Sessions commuted from his Princeton home to teach at Juilliard and stayed Tuesday nights at the Hotel Empire. He continued this schedule until 1983. While I was sharing an office with Sessions, the idea of writing about a living composer lurked in the back of my mind. Working on a short article for *Current Musicology* entitled "American Music at Juilliard" proved providential. Because the school had several distinguished American composers on its faculty and administration, I interviewed three of them on the subject of American music: Peter Mennin, Stanley Wolfe, and Elliott Carter. Juilliard had commissioned two works from Sessions, the Piano Concerto as well as the Double Concerto, and it had performed his opera *The Trial of Lucullus* in 1966. I worked up my courage to approach Sessions, who still looked rather formidable, and finally spoke to him: "Mr. Sessions, I'd like to ask you some questions about American music." This was in a hallway. He replied, "Oh, my dear, that would take all day." Not daring to pursue this because a day of his valuable time seemed too much to ask, I retreated.

Having scouted the bibliography, I was surprised to learn that, considering his fame, no one had yet devoted a book to him. I asked one of Sessions's former students, William Komaiko, to invite me to lunch with the two of them. In May of 1974 the three of us had a long lunch and, after Mr. Sessions left (we all called him that, no matter how close we eventually became to him), I announced simply, "I'm going to write about him." In person, his charm, honesty, and youthfulness had reversed the austere image of him I had retained for three years. He was straightforward, insightful, and totally human. At the time Sessions was seventy-seven years old and I was twenty-five.

The appropriate method seemed to me to be the tape-recorded interview format of oral history, although no one in musicology was then doing this. (Vivian Perlis's oral history on Ives was published that fall and gave me the comforting feeling of not being alone.) In September 1974 I told Sessions of my plans to write a book about his music and audaciously asked if I could interview him every week for the next two years! He agreed, and we set our first appointment for when school started in October. I borrowed a tape recorder (I could not afford to buy one), bought cheap tapes, and read everything I could find about him. The Juilliard library and record library kept up on the school's composers. In fact, this library is one of the most complete repositories of Sessions's scores and recordings.

To the appointments themselves. Sessions had moved to Room 509B, fifteen yards away from Room 516. This was a small room with only a grand piano, a desk, a closet, and a window to adorn it. For our interviews Sessions always sat at the desk. After quickly plugging in the tape recorder and setting up a microphone, I took what seemed a logical approach: I tackled his works in chronological order with a list of prepared questions, supported by relevant scores.

In answer to direct questions Sessions would often start a long, seemingly totally unrelated story that would only after much time turn out to have a bearing on the question. At first I did not realize this and interpreted his extremely long pauses as conclusions but later learned not to comment even when he seemed finished—he was still thinking and would speak again. Eventually in the course of the hour he would get to what really concerned him, although that might not be the music on the agenda. For example, during the 1975–76 year, when the Opera Company of Boston was producing *Montezuma,* almost all questions led to a discussion of this opera. For Sessions, certain pieces, or people, were "very much on my mind" at different times.

Evidently Sessions also enjoyed our weekly encounters. After the two years were completed, and for each of four years following, he would say, "We still have a lot to talk about," and I was eager to continue. Often he would look at music, photographs, or reviews that he had either forgotten about or never seen. Here was a formal opportunity to look back at his earlier music from a considerable distance. He then recalled whatever had lodged in his memory: where he was on the day he received a commission, the hall in which a piece was performed, getting the first idea for the piece, and other associations.

During one early interview, when I was switching the cassette tape to the other side, Sessions said, "I got one of those cassette recorders to dictate my autobiography informally, and I haven't even gotten it out of the box yet. I've had it for seven months." When asked if he were going to write his autobiography, he replied: "I'm not going to write a thing. I'm just going to make some tapes so that certain things will be there for my children and anybody who wanted to write it. Discretion isn't my middle name, because it doesn't go well with my last name. That's one thing that makes it difficult, and the other thing that makes it difficult is that one begins reminiscing, you know. And there are a lot of things that are much more interesting to oneself than they possibly could be to anyone else."

Sessions never did dictate his autobiography, although clearly he had intended to do so. Perhaps he thought that our weekly taped interviews were an appropriate substitute. During the last eleven years of his life I was the only author or interviewer who worked on his biography and interviewed him regularly (despite a cryptic assertion by Barry Brook in *The Music Makers* about a Sessions project at C.U.N.Y.)

The differences between us in age and sex turned out to be unimportant, but our viewpoints and training mirrored fundamentally different approaches to music. As one of the century's great composers, Sessions viewed music in the macrocosm; whereas I had been trained as a violinist and a musicologist to examine it only in the microcosm. The narrow search for where the notes actually came from was met with frustration. But my education was only beginning.

Sessions frequently invoked composers from the great classical tradition. This occasionally took a humorous form, as when the mention of Bach elicited the comment, "He was one of our best men." He was careful to avoid negative remarks about his contemporaries or about younger composers, although on one rare occasion he expressed the opinion that Ives was overrated. He inveighed about composers who spoke against fellow composers; he considered this particularly inappropriate behavior for artists.

Sessions took the long view. His generalities seemed to betray an unwillingness to deal specifically with composition. Regarding his twelve-tone music, even so simple a question as "What is the row?" always met with a lengthy and anecdotal monologue about the unimportance of the twelve-tone technique; what was important was the music. Since the rows in Sessions's music are often not immediately apparent, and I felt that this knowledge would aid future analysts of his music, I pressed him. Once, in what might be construed a weak moment, he explained the row and its alteration in his cantata. Fortunately, I had the score to the Double Concerto along that day and seized the opportunity to locate specific statements of the row there as well.

Obviously, Sessions possessed the ability to be extremely specific about composition and had been so in the past as a teacher, according to his former students. However, as Edward T. Cone observed in a review,[1] in the last decades of his life Sessions had acquired a "pronounced anti-analytical bias." He discarded common musical terms such as "theme," "sonata form," "twelve-tone," preferring to speak of "craftsmanship," or "gestures." (To combat his expected generalities I would occasionally adopt an extreme position in order to get a more concrete reaction, as for instance, on the subject of *Parsifal*.) Of course, he was trying to convey a deeper level of understanding, one to which decades of composing had led him. This was at first hard for me, a non-composer, to grasp. However, after weeks stretched into years and I had written articles and the proposed book[2] about him, his words frequently echoed in my mind as apt and true.

I compare the experience of learning from Sessions to having formerly looked at music through a microscope and now seeing it through a telescope. For me an opposition was set up between the views of music found at a conservatory (where I taught and which Sessions represented) and the views of music prevailing in university graduate schools (where I was trained and with which Sessions was associated in the minds of the press). Each had something to recommend it—the scholarship of academia and the performance orientation of a conservatory. Under the influence of a powerful and persuasive personality, the balance tipped for me decisively in favor of Sessions and the conservatory view.

Consider a historical question: Which is more "true," what the composer remembers, or what actually happened? On the one hand, Sessions's memory was astounding. In preparing his family tree I asked for dates of birth of unaccounted-for distant aunts, uncles, or cousins. He remembered *all* of them perfectly confidently. On the other hand, events that were unpleasant were quite humanly repressed. For example, in answering questions about the locations of his manuscripts, he said that the manuscript for the First Symphony was either destroyed or lost. Later I located the manuscript, deposited in 1980 at the Houghton Library at Harvard as part of Nadia Boulanger's bequest. Evidently Sessions chose to forget that Boulanger—with whom there had been a breach—had possessed the manuscript for over fifty years.

The issue of the validity of oral history still concerned me, even though I carefully checked as much information as possible. Since Sessions was often the only source on the subject of Sessions, I was keenly aware of "creating" the record of which this book consists. Indeed, I occasionally felt that I was interrupting history when, for example, Sessions was composing in his studio before our appointment. The years of our interviews saw the creation of the Five Pieces for Piano, the Waltz, the Ninth Symphony, and the Concerto for Orchestra. It was particularly exciting to discuss pieces in progress, as he showed me sketches and completed pages.

Another issue was maintaining a critical distance from a subject with whom I became increasingly involved personally. Weekly appointments were augmented by our attendance at concerts and parties together, as well as frequent lunches and dinners, and yearly birthday lunches for him given by his students and myself. I was also fortunate to be able to listen to rehearsals when performers played his music for him. We spent a great deal of time discussing concerts we had attended. When separated in summers, we frequently wrote, although he was not otherwise a good correspondent. Although at first Sessions was rather formal—he addressed me as "Miss Olmstead" for two years—he later called me his "confidante," an accurate description of our relationship. This went both ways: When I became romantically involved with a composition student of Vincent Persichetti's, Larry Bell, Sessions and his close friend Persichetti became personally concerned about our relationship and were delighted by our marriage. Mr. Persichetti encouraged Larry to take a few composition lessons from Sessions, which he did, as well as taking Sessions's doctoral course at Juilliard. During that year, 1979–80, our four lives very much intermingled.

As is well known, Sessions did nothing to promote

recordings or performances of his own music; he merely waited for performers to approach it on their own. It seemed often as though that were taking too long a time to occur. Throughout his eighty-eight-year life he always took the "long view." Blessed with good health and with an overview that reached far into the past as well as into the future, he was able to maintain the poise of infinite patience such as few of us can claim.

These *Conversations* are strictly conversational: Sessions spoke casually—although the casual and the formal were almost identical in him. None of his words here were written out ahead of time, nor were any of his memories of music prepared. His openness with me in our interviews led to his revealing private information never intended to be made public. The following *Conversations* took place weekly between 1974 and 1980 and are edited as to content and, of course, to make them more readable.

Nevertheless, I would like this book to portray as accurately as possible what these conversations were like: his roundabout way of answering questions, the vast knowledge of repertoire that he possessed, his political awareness, his aversion to technical terms dealing with music, his sense of humor and kindness, and his subtle sense of his own importance without an accompanying air of pompousness. Unfortunately, the written word cannot also convey his deep, slow-paced voice, his frequent laughter, his singing to illustrate points, his sympathy and tenderness toward his family and friends, the number of times he mentioned his wife, Lisl, or his youthfulness. Nor does it convey his nervous habits of continually cleaning and refilling his pipe and shuffling papers.

While reading over and commenting on a part of my

manuscript where I quoted him, Sessions observed, "Of course, a lot of these things that I say about this really have to do with the differences between saying something and then having it in print. Because when it is in print, it's without any nuance at all." (Years earlier, my musicology professor at Juilliard, Gustave Reese, had observed, "One cannot write prose polyphonically; one can only write monophonically.")

To those who knew him—and there were many students and friends over the years—perhaps a typical "Sessionsism" of speech in these *Conversations* will evoke a smile of recognition. To those who did not come into contact with him, the *Conversations* will provide a picture of a very human, enormously cultivated, and unpretentious man, who was also one of America's greatest composers.

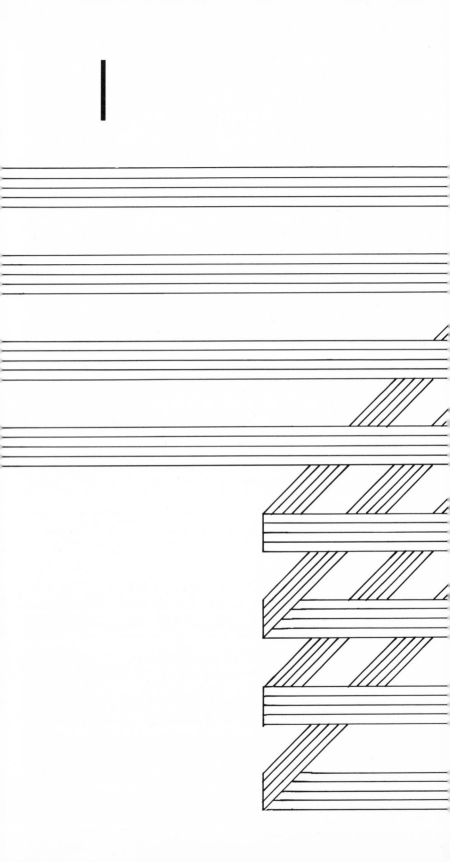

Orchestral

Music

I suppose all my life I've thought for the orchestra. And then next to that, I suppose I've thought for the piano, because I do play the piano. But I had to learn to think of the piano as an instrument aside from something I play just for convenience. In all my extant piano works, I've thought of the piano as a color, and of all the colors I can get from the piano.

Composers use the piano for their own purposes, of course, but I never compose at the piano. My first piece, *Lancelot and Elaine,* was conceived while I was on a bicycle. I wouldn't have a piano till I'd been to the dentist five miles away and come back from the dentist. But I put it all down when I got home. I wasn't aware that I was composing earlier, but I made up tunes. I made up tunes to words, especially.

Could you tell me something about your earliest catalogued piece, The Black Maskers?

The Black Maskers was written originally for a very small, scratch orchestra for a performance of the play at Smith College in 1923. It's a very strange play, and I don't wholly get it yet. It was a Russian play translated into English. I didn't choose the play myself, although it's very striking in a way. It has dramatic possibilities.

Smith College is in the town where I spent my childhood for about six years. Then I went back and taught there for four years. I saw this man, Samuel Eliot, Jr., whom I'd already known at Harvard. He directed the theater at Smith. The tradition was that each year the senior class put on a Shakespeare play, but they wanted to get away from Shakespeare. I was out in Cleveland at the time, and I got a telegram asking me if I would write the music for *The Black Maskers*. I'd read the play before. It's a strange play; it's about an Italian Renaissance nobleman who's the son of a Crusader, supposedly. And he comes upon a document which convinces him that he is really the offspring of an affair that his mother had with a groom, probably. The husband had been away at the Crusades. And that unhinges him, as far as his sense of identity is concerned, and it's highly symbolical. There are five scenes.

The first scene, he's put on a big party, and all the guests come in strange masks. The first movement of the suite I made from this music. I went to town with the orchestra, which I couldn't do with the Incidental Music. There are all sorts of bizarre episodes during this dance. Gradually the orchestra breaks up into complete chaos.

There's nothing of the second scene in the suite. I wrote the whole orchestral accompaniment to it, but not very much goes on, it's not to be played by itself. The main character, Lorenzo, is up in his tower poring over these documents, and he's confronted by his double. I guess the double is the rational side of his nature. Or maybe the double is the irrational side. Anyway, they have a duel, and the irrational prince Lorenzo kills the rational side.

And he goes back down to the ballroom, and by that time a whole lot of strange black creatures have come in. And every time they come in, the lights dim a little more. (I don't have the whole music to this scene in the suite.) Finally the music fades out, but Lorenzo, the one who's alive, sees all this chaos going on, and he sort of hums a wistful tune for a moment. The black maskers, these strange black creatures that he sees, take the trumpets of the onstage orchestral players and trumpet wildly.

When I made the suite, I filled in the gap between the fading out of the music and the wild trumpeting at the end. More or less, I tried to follow the development of this scene as it is in the play. I have the tune that he hums. (The girl who sang it couldn't possibly do it; she also couldn't do the song in the first act.) The transformation occurs during this song. The song, "My soul is an enchanted castle" ends up as an invocation to Satan. That's in the suite, too, although Romualdo's Song isn't always performed with it.

You have a note in the score that it could be omitted.

Yes. That is exactly as I wrote it for the Smith production for this small group. It's been often performed separately, and sometimes performed with the suite. Of course, it's for a soprano. In the play it's a man singer, but since this was performed by girls, I wrote it for soprano. The character was named Romualdo, and so it's called "Romualdo's Song."

For the song that Lorenzo hums, the only instrument I could think of was the alto flute, which was a fairly uncommon instrument at that time. It's no problem nowadays at all.

Then the fourth scene: The *dead* Lorenzo is in his coffin, and in the play there is a sort of vague chanting going on by monks in the background. In the performance I improvised on a little reed organ behind the scenes. You see, all this had to be done behind the scenes. It didn't work very well, but the director was awfully distressed

when I said that we'd got to have the orchestra in the
pit. He said, "It would spoil my production, but I'll do it
if you want." And I said, "Well, we'll go on as it is."
Rather amusing occasion, because I sat improvising these
sorts of pseudo-medieval, quasi-Gregorian things on the
organ. Well now, in the suite, I put just the beginning
of that. And in the beginning of the scene there are these
trumpets that are supposed to announce the death of
Lorenzo from the tower, or the battlements of the castle,
and in the suite it's just the orchestral introduction to
the scene that's called "Dirge." The dirge is the same
music as in the Incidental Music, but it's for full orchestra instead of a little orchestra. I reinforced everything
very much.

In the last scene you have another ball. And this is the
part I just don't get in the play. One of the characters is
a jester who's a hunchback, and everybody teases him
and he teases them back—he has a sharp tongue. But
again, they're getting ready for a ball, and the ball comes
and the guests come; the Lorenzo who appears is insane.
I made an unaccompanied song at this point. It's much
less important than the one in the first act, much less
related to the development as a whole. The jester has set
fire to the castle, and Lorenzo dies in the flames. He is
redeemed somehow by being burnt up by the fire of his
own castle. I don't quite get it; it's not my idea of
redemption exactly.

Isn't that the same idea as in Die Götterdämmerung?

Yes, I suppose. The *Götterdämmerung* started it. That's
what the last movement is, anyway. In the first version
the last movement is much simpler, because the kinds of

things I'd like to have done weren't possible with the bunch that played it, the change of meters, and so forth.

How do the versions of the finale differ?

I think I tightened it up more and more. I did all the things that I didn't dare do with that scratch orchestra. Much more brilliant work for the violins, and four horns instead of one, four trumpets instead of two, and three trombones and tuba, and then lots of woodwinds, and they could do things like this. I changed the meters when I felt like it, which I couldn't have done for that performance either, you see.

You evidently prefer the B-flat trumpet, although it isn't as common as the C.

C trumpets are more convenient for some people, but I like the tone of the B-flat trumpet better; the C trumpet's a little thin. Of course, the trumpet I really like is obsolete now because it was too difficult to play. It's the old F trumpet—wonderful tone! It was so hard that orchestras very often substituted cornets for them. The cornet is a perfectly good instrument, but it is nothing like a trumpet, because it has a conical tube instead of a cylindrical one and a more hybrid tone. I like that old trumpet in F so much that I thought at one time I'd like to make propaganda to bring it back into the orchestra. It's impossible. I even owned one once, and I gave it to a very, very good trumpeter in the Philadelphia Orchestra. It's got a wonderful, rich tone—I used to say it's got a tone like white light. There was no yellow carbon in the light at all. It's a wonderful sound, and when you hear Siegfried's funeral march from the *Götterdämmerung,* or the funeral march from the *Eroica,* or the prelude to *Parsifal,* it just sends the shivers down your back.

> *There's an article by Elliott Carter about you in which he describes this period, around 1923, as Impressionistic.* [1]

He said there's something in it, but there isn't very much. The only rather abrupt change that came in my music was just after *The Black Maskers.* I felt that there were some things about *The Black Maskers* that I didn't accomplish as I wanted to. A harmonic limitation. I couldn't make my harmonies move in the way I wanted, the kinds of harmonies I was using. The emphasis was on the short motivic lines. This appeared to me much more magnified than it seems now. I quite like *The Black Maskers* still. But I wanted to get away from complicated psychology and symbolism.

> *The play seemed to me more Expressionistic than Impressionistic.*

Of course, I don't really know what either of these words means. I can recognize some of the things. But why *La Mer* is more impressionistic than the *Pastoral* Symphony, I don't know. The music is quite different, but . . . I understand that Expressionism really meant heightening every moment to the utmost. I think it's wrongly applied to Schoenberg and Berg. I think these titles apply to the inferior music of every period. I mean,

Debussy was *much* more than an Impressionist. I would say, too, that Bach was much more than a baroque composer. These things apply to the epigones, not to the people. All I would say is that I think works of art are basically unique. And each one has its own character, and I'm not interested in classifications.

What inspired you to write the First Symphony?

Actually, I wanted to write a piano quintet. I wasn't always satisfied with the first idea. Then I realized that I was thinking of an orchestral piece instead. I sketched a hundred different versions of the first idea, just systematically. And then I realized that one of them was much better than the others, and curiously enough, that was the simplest one. I was surprised, because it seemed extremely simple, but yet it was the best one.

Parts of the score reminded me of Stravinsky or Milhaud.

It's very much the influence of Stravinsky, although it's not really like Stravinsky at all. It's a different kind of music, but I certainly was influenced by Stravinsky very, very strongly.

There seems to be an affinity with Stravinsky's rhythm.

Yes. Except the rhythm is different, too. It's a sort of metrical freedom which I've always had, although once I wanted to get away from it. I was afraid it was becoming a formula and I tried in a certain sense to rid myself of *that,* you see.

Originally I wrote this in much smaller measures. I'd write 3/8, 4/8, and 5/8, and sometimes even 2/8. That seemed to me the most logical way to do it. But when Koussevitsky conducted it, he wanted to combine these measures, and he went through with a blue pencil and put in measures. Well, he put them in the wrong place, from my point of view. So after the performance, I went over it and put the measures where I thought they belonged. Then a curious thing happened. Koussevitsky said, "You never could conduct that this way, with those small measures." Afterwards Ansermet played it; he gave an excellent performance in Geneva, and then he played it in Berlin with a second-rate orchestra. He was having a hard time, because at that time it was a very difficult work. A very difficult work. In fact, Klemperer told me he wouldn't dare conduct it.

The brass certainly have difficult parts.

Well, they were difficult *then*. They're not difficult now at all. In fact, as far as I know, the Princeton student orchestra is going to play it next week. They've had some difficulties; they said they might have to postpone it, but so far there's been no postponement. So that's not difficult today. I've conducted it myself.

I asked Ansermet if there was anything I could do to make it easier, and he said, "No, no. You can't simplify the truth." But he said, "Maybe if you wrote smaller measures it would be easier. Instead of writing an 8/8 measure with 3 + 2 + 3, you wrote 3/8, 2/8, and 3/8."

I told him what had led to making them the larger measures, and he threw up his hands. I make larger measures regularly now, but these present not that much difficulty today. At least, I don't think they do.

> *All the articles I read about this piece mentioned the rhythmic innovations as the one greatest contribution, or most advanced style element, of the piece.*

I didn't think of it as innovating, but that's the way I thought the movement had to go, and some of my ideas simply took that shape in the beginning. Even the syncopations. Of course, Koussevitsky would have liked me to write the whole thing in 2/4 time and put accents in. But an accent is quite different from a downbeat. These three measures [beginning at rehearsal number 7] correspond exactly to these two measures here [two measures before rehearsal number 8], and are identical except in some details of orchestration. But here they are three measures in 2/4 time, and here they are 3 + 3 + 2 + 4, and this stresses the differences between syncopations and accents on the beat. I didn't get *that* from Stravinsky.

Many of these changes of meter came from my awareness of that distinction. I sketched a lot of this in 2/4 time. (I never told Koussevitsky that.) But sometimes, in certain cases, when I wrote the work, I would shorten a measure, take out an eighth. This, for instance, originally came on the second beat (you know, I haven't thought of this from that day to this), but I realized that this should be a downbeat here [at rehearsal number 10 trumpet part]. In other cases, I felt that a note like that was too long, and so I shortened the measure. And these ideas over here [three measures before rehearsal number 14] were originally written in 2/4 time, but it's really 3 + 2 + 3 instead of 4 + 4, so I combined them in a measure.

Some passages like this [at rehearsal number 10] struck me as similar to Milhaud's interpretation of jazz. Did you think in terms of jazz here?

I never thought consciously in terms of jazz. Naturally, I heard a lot of it, and I feel that both in this movement and the last movement there is a certain trace of jazz. And curiously enough, when people hear this work nowadays, it's that that strikes them more than any relation to Stravinsky. Ragtime became jazz just at about the same time as I was writing the symphony. Jazz was something very, very, new. It was a new word.

Can you tell me why you say "jazz" rather than "ragtime?"

Well, if you'll tell me the difference between them.

I don't know. I was going to ask you. [laughter]

I think that they just suddenly began calling it jazz, that's all. I think (this isn't anything beyond a guess) that when people began to be a little self-conscious about syncopation and that sort of thing, they began calling it something special. Jazz, actually. For instance, there was a popular piece, it was just a C major scale, played in a way they called "ragging the scale." That was a late precursor, or early example, of jazz. That was in the twenties sometime.

Jazz had some influence from Impressionism.

Listen, everything influenced this. When I finally came back from Europe in 1933, I felt that the popular music that I was hearing all sounded like Ravel. Of course, jazz and ragtime have influenced European composers. Milhaud you spoke of wrote a ragtime piece called *La Création du Monde*. And Stravinsky wrote *Piano Rag Music* and ragtime in the teens and early twenties, and then that particular phase didn't last very long. After that it was the so-called classical music that began influencing popular composers here.

Much has been made of your concept of the "long line." The second movement is a largo movement. How do you manage to escape cadences and phrase endings for such a long time?

Well, I just let it work itself out.

The first place I could determine an end of a phrase comes after four pages [two bars after rehearsal number 55].

On the other hand, you could say that one phrase ends here [at rehearsal number 51] and another phrase begins with the violins, and then the violas come in with another phrase [rehearsal number 52], and then finally the cellos come in.

But it's basically the same phrase.

Oh, yes, it's the same, but it's built up. It's one whole unit. Incidentally, the recording of the first movement is much too fast. It should be played not staccato, but tenuto, by the brass. I was worried about that recording. It was made in Japan, and there was nothing I could do about it. It was originally 116–120 to the quarter, but one has to be careful because one reads music and thinks it so much faster than one can listen to it or than one can play it clearly. One of the metronome marks in my second piano sonata is much, much too fast. I was appalled when the pianist played it for me, and I said, "But that's much too fast." He sort of giggled and took the printed score out and the metronome mark was much too fast. That 116 is the real tempo for this symphony, and it has to be played tenuto.

Which would give it less of a Stravinsky quality. On the record it sounded more like Stravinsky because of the accentuation and the staccato, I find.

Probably. That may be. You may be quite right. I never thought of that. But you may very well be quite right about that.

The reviews of the Spivakovsky performance of the Violin Concerto in 1959 were very good. It is a shame that it had to wait twenty-five years.

25

That, my dear Andrea, is what musical life is like in America and, above all, in New York nowadays. It's a matter of dollars and cents. It is a matter of "stars" who may be first-class performers, and who may not be. It's a matter of a public that really is afraid to let itself go but wants to be "sophisticated." You know what I'm talking about.

I do. But waiting twenty-five years for a performance with a major orchestra!

Well, you know, Johann Sebastian Bach had to wait even longer. And he was really one of our best men. [laughter]

When you mentioned the lack of violins [in the scoring], it occurred to me that in 1930 Stravinsky wrote his Symphony of Psalms *in which he eliminates the violins. Is it possible that his piece presented a possible route to take?*

It might have, but I don't think I'd heard the *Symphony of Psalms* at that time. I could have. The main thing was that I didn't want to have my violin covered by a whole sea of violins, too.

It also occurred to me, contrasting the Piano Concerto with the Violin Concerto, that in this piece the violin almost always has the main musical line and almost always plays, whereas the Piano Concerto strikes me more

as an equal dialogue between the piano and the or-
chestra.

But, you see, the piano is generally not an orchestral instrument, although it has been in a good deal of my music.

Is this a reason for giving the piano more of a dialogue character, sometimes subsidiary to the orchestral line?

Well, one doesn't think of those things beforehand. One's writing a piece of music.

I noticed that a lot of the Violin Concerto stayed on the E string, which of course makes it sound more brilliant and piercing, but it's very high in register.

Of course that also jibes with my not having violins in the orchestra.

Is this the only instance when you use the bassett horn?

Yes. Generally it's played on the alto clarinet, which is perfectly good. And in the New York performance they got a real bassett horn player from outside, who I sup- pose never played anything except the Mozart *Requiem*, perhaps an eighteenth-century suite or something like that. I know why I used it; because Strauss uses bassett horns in *Elektra*. That's how I got the idea. I assumed that it would probably be easy to get a player, but those parts are probably played on alto clarinets, too. You have to have the bassett horn in this piece. That may be one reason it hasn't been played more often.

I wanted to have as many different varieties of woodwinds as possible. And I used the alto flute, and piccolo. I used two English horns at first instead of two oboes. I used the contrabassoon. I think it was the tones of the woodwinds that I wanted to emphasize in this, and that's why I left out the violins. I wanted to play the woodwinds off against the soloist.

The reason Koussevitsky didn't play any more of my music after the episode with Spalding and the Violin Concerto was this: This orchestra, which was conducted by Koussevitsky's nephew, whom he didn't like—he was very jealous of him—played *The Black Maskers*. I have a letter in my files from Koussevitsky. I think it's in connection with the Violin Concerto. He said, "By the way, I see that a work of yours is scheduled by this other orchestra. And I think you should know that composers whose works are played by that orchestra don't appear on the programs of the Boston Symphony."

What did he have against this other orchestra?

It was conducted by his nephew; it was another orchestra in Boston. The Boston Symphony did not play my music under him after that. (I don't want to be seen as attacking another musician.)

The Second Symphony was sort of the first really big success I had. In a way my First Symphony was, too, but not in the same way. This was played in San Francisco and conducted by Monteux. And then, two years after that, it was conducted by Mitropoulos with the Philharmonic here, and recorded. The recording has just been reissued [by CRI], and it sounds like hell, if I may say so.

The older one is good. I would have liked to have ideally Mitropoulos playing the first and third movements and Monteux playing the second and the fourth movements. I wish I had called the second movement "Intermezzo," because that's really what it is. It's not a full-fledged scherzo at all. It's a very short, and a somewhat light, interlude between a stormy first movement and a very dark slow movement.

Andrew Imbrie's article[2] discusses the first chord's reappearance at the beginning of each of the five sections of the first movement.

He found it in places where I wasn't aware that it was. When you're composing, you have certain sounds in your ears, which are identified with that piece. They do come back. He finds it here at letter Dd, for instance. I didn't connect it in my mind with this music, but it is of course.

Henry Cowell[3] points out a certain serial technique involved in the movement. I took the initial themes of each of the four movements and looked for something that could resemble a row. And indeed I found one.

That was totally unconscious, because I was still somewhat stubbornly against the row. I wasn't against it, I was against it for me. I didn't feel that it applied to my music at all. It was seven years later that I used the row for the first time.

The fourth movement seems to me to have a very rondo-like character.

Or rondo-sonata. As I told you, I don't mind what folder you put it in.

It seems that this rhythmic pattern was so characteristic and I felt it was foreshadowed earlier [on page 37 of the score].

I don't think I was aware of that, but it's there. Of course, these middle movements were written quite a bit before the others. A lot of this was sketched around the time I was working on the Duo. The second movement was originally going to be one of the *Pages from a Diary,* and I decided that I didn't want it to be a piano piece. I decided that it was in a different mood from the others. I made some very slight changes toward the end—I don't remember exactly what. I didn't make it any longer, but I think these measures [at letter L] were different. This development [at letter K] was different. I really sketched this all at one sitting, but not with all the details, obviously.

Until my Fifth Symphony all my symphonies had pauses. My Fifth and Eighth are the only ones which don't. I haven't decided about number nine yet, but that might not have pauses, too.

How do you make these decisions? For instance, the second string quartet doesn't have pauses, as well as some other pieces which are also fairly lengthy and are large forms. When do you decide to connect two movements, through, say, one instrument?

I suppose the music itself and the general feeling of design. I don't know.

There isn't anything sacrosanct about the form of the symphony.

I don't think there is any such thing as the symphony. I mean, there are symphonies. The symphony is a matter for filing cabinets, you know. I think filing cabinets are essentially irrelevant to the musical question.

I felt that there were connections among the movements of the Third Symphony. They were separated and contrasted, but the original material of the first movement was brought back in each of the other three movements.

Yes. Of course, I had a kind of design in my mind when I wrote this. And I have a lot of human associations. Koussevitsky was a very warm man, a very touchy man. And at a certain point there was a kind of breach between us, I told you about. One of the conditions of the commission was that it be dedicated to the memory of Serge and Natalie Koussevitsky.

The place where Koussevitsky is buried is in the courtyard of a little church at the top of a hill in Lenox. It's really quite a lovely place, with trees around it. I thought of the third movement up there. But there were many other things going on in my life at the same time, and as I was writing this, a lot of them come in as associations. Well, that's true with all my music. But I don't consider that the music is committed to them at all. There are associations which had some influence on the work. It's a very personal work, and at the same time, it's the nearest thing to an orthodox symphony that any of my symphonies are. I don't know the reason for that. It was a sort of a challenge. The nearest thing in my adult years I wrote to the sonata form is the last movement. It's not quite a sonata form.

There is a row, which I use more thematically than otherwise, because I was approaching the twelve-tone system easily and naturally. And this is less orthodox in that respect than in some of my other works of that time. The row is the basis of one of the ideas in the last movement. Cross my heart and hope to die, not until the very end did I realize that it ends in a sort of tonic and dominant, dominant and tonic. And I had a lot of fun writing those last measures, because at the very end that comes out. Not that the tonic has been prepared tonally at all, but that's the way the symphony ends. You have $A^\flat$ and $D^\flat$ in the timpani and trombones, and so you have a descending fifth at the end. That was not a joke exactly, but it was fun.

How long did it take you to write this, once you had thought of it?

Well, it took me a long time, because I had all the main ideas of all the movements two or three years before I was even asked to write it. I was working on something else—perhaps on my quartet—in California. And one morning I thought of this first idea of the first movement and the idea of the second movement. I wrote out a sketch for all of this, the beginning of the slow movement, and the beginning of the last movement. And I thought, "Well, that's the next symphony I'm going to write." It happened in the fall of '52 in California, because I remember sitting at my desk. I had several ideas for works that I was going to write later on at that time. My Fourth Symphony, too. But I put them aside. I knew "that's a work I'm going to write someday." And then when the Boston Symphony asked me to write a symphony in memory of Koussevitsky, that came naturally. Of course, those were only the initial ideas of various movements. I knew what I was going to do. That doesn't happen always. But in that particular case, that did happen. I wrote them all at one sitting. Thought of the whole work. The ideas didn't come out in exactly the same form. Although I think in the last movement and in the second movement, they did. The slow movement was the least definite, as I remember it. I'm not absolutely sure of that.

It was begun probably in '55, a little. I know '55 was the summer I spent in Tanglewood. But I had my Mass on my hands, and I had my Piano Concerto on my hands. I couldn't get started on this till I finished both of those things. This I really got going on in the fall of '56, and I didn't finish it till a year later. It's the longest and the biggest of all my symphonies. I'm very curious about how Boulez happened to choose this one [for the New York Philharmonic performance in 1976].

I was looking for the row in the Fourth Symphony.

I'm not sure I could find it. The row is very tenuous in the piece, I think. You see at that time, I didn't want to depend on the row for any thematic material. The row plays a very secondary role in this piece.

If the themes were not derived from the row, then would you say that the vertical harmonies were?

Sometimes, but of course, I forget the row always afterwards. It's very important when I'm working. Even Webern, who's supposed to be the arch-apostle of the row as such, talked that way very often. That's where he and Schoenberg differed. Webern wouldn't tell people who played his music what the row was. He said, "The row is how the piece is made, but your job is to know how it should be played."

The first movement is a sort of sonata form.

Sort of, yes, with deviations. But I think the recapitulation is somewhat regular. That's what I would judge by. Although never is the recapitulation literal—the episodes return, but they're always changed somewhat. And very often the texture is recalled instrumentally without being the same music exactly. If you can call it a coda—it's so short—it would come here at measure 144, eight measures long in the solo violin. It's a sort of a little parody of my Second Symphony.

This big section at the opening of the second movement has led some people to speak of it as the slow movement. In a sense, it has the character of an exposition.

How long did it take you to write it from the time you first started?

The "Pastorale"? Well, I had it all completely sketched, and I even made some of these sketches in my mind without writing it down. Then it didn't take me very long to work it out. Probably I wrote it very quickly. You see, I made a trip to Russia in the meantime. This was interrupted, delayed. I had to tell them it would be delayed. And they said, "Your commission won't be fulfilled unless you get it finished by the end of the year." I wrote the very beginning of the slow movement in the Soviet Union. Probably these two opening pages in Moscow. I didn't have much time, and the working conditions weren't very ideal, the circumstances. Because here I was in a new place, and I was curious. I got started on the "Pastorale" there. And I had a pencil sketch and then I copied it out.

When the first performance of my Second Symphony was given in San Francisco, my daughter was six years old. We took her to the concert. The orchestra was very good. And my daughter turned to my wife and said, "Is that daddy's music? It's very pretty." I told Mitropoulos about that; he liked my Second Symphony very much. He said, "Tell your daughter that I agree with her." See, I forget these things, if I don't look at them for a while. Now it all comes back to me.

What specifically is recalled about the Second Symphony in the Fourth Symphony? Is it a mood in particular?

On the contrary. It's a very noisy and dramatic piece. Only resemblance here is a little with tongue in one cheek. It wasn't anything very specific, but when I wrote that violin solo, I thought to myself, "Well, here we have a little violin solo," but it's meant in a much lighter and more satirical sense. I mean, this is really a "Burlesque."

So, it's the first movement that you feel is the parody of the Second Symphony?

Oh, yes, not any of the rest. I planned these pieces with the "Elegy," the first one I thought of, and then I thought, "What other pieces can I put with this?" I thought of just the names of the three Greek forms of drama. Just the names, because the Greek pastoral plays were plays about peasants. My "Pastorale" had nothing to do with farmers. It's more my feelings about Nature. And I wasn't at every moment thinking, "This is a parody," I was just following the music where it seemed to lead.

Can you remember any other pieces that you've written that you considered parodies of anyone else besides yourself?

No, just this particular instance. That's the way it turned out. I didn't think of this before the fact at all. I just knew I was writing a piece somewhat in the spirit of a burlesque, that's all.

Now, maybe there's more of the twelve-tone in this than I remember. Because I remember in my quintet, which came just before the Fourth Symphony, that I had felt that I used the twelve-tone system in a more thoroughgoing way than I'd ever used it before. And I felt that there was somewhat of a difference that came there in my music. Of course, it's a matter of medium. You have to learn to do these things in various mediums. You use them as the medium seems to require, or not use them. There's a difference in texture.

How does that difference in texture affect the treatment?

When you have three, four, or five lines, then you don't have so many tones at a time. And when you have a heavier texture, you get rid of the notes much more quickly; for instance, the twelve-tone series. If you want to get the variety that you need, things have to change more rapidly. It's a question of economy. In a larger piece you have to organize the twelve tones differently. The whole tempo at which the row appears becomes somewhat different. Not that things in the music happen quickly, but you use up all the twelve tones more quickly. And if you want to use a transposition at a certain point—you don't want to use it here—then you have to use the same row over and over again. If I come into New York, I've got to be sure I've got enough one- and five-dollar bills. But when I'm in Princeton and go shopping the town, or pay bills, I don't have to worry about the one-dollar bills so much. [laughter] That's in a way the gist of it.

You don't have only *one* line of sixteenth notes, for instance; you may have three lines going together. If each sixteenth then uses three notes of the series, just in one beat, you've used up all twelve notes. I'd probably have to go into enormous and unsystematic sounding detail in order to make the whole procedure clear, and it would take me years to do that, and I wouldn't dream of doing it. Just remember, the music is God and the twelve-tone technique is just a parish priest.

> *After hearing the performance of your Sixth Symphony so many things seemed much clearer than they did in the rehearsals. It seems to me that the connections in the piece are concentrated; for example, two notes would recur, or a rhythm, or a certain kind of texture. But they seemed fleeting in our time sense today; we're used to long chunks of recapitulation.*

There are more connections than that. The last movement almost has no theme at all, except the trumpet call at the beginning, which comes back, of course. It does have a theme, but it's treated so freely that it's the general style and the mood. The first movement of course has that figure at the beginning, and then there are passages that correspond. I think when you get to know the work better you'll see them. For instance, these measures here [measures 5–6] are answered in the strings. At measure 155 the material does come back, but there's constant development. The piano figure is not what's important at measure 115, it's the violas. You have reminiscences, but in quite different form in all my music from the Third Symphony on. It's a more static recalling of the same ideas.

> *This had the feeling of constant activity to me. I had the feeling of concentration of materials.*

That's true from *Montezuma* on. In this style, recapitulation in the old sense of the word would not work at all. The way to recapitulate is by change. For instance in the Seventh Symphony, there's always movement ahead. The movement you might say is planned on dynamic terms as a whole. Of course, I think that was true of the older music, too, but it's a different style. When it's a question of keys coming back, you have a quite different problem, because you're not returning to the same key, to the same tonal center.

Essentially, it's always a question of variation, you see. It's the same material, but it's variation within a certain framework. It's not so free as a set of variations, because they all have a certain character in common. The variations are simply the vehicle for the form. It's not variation 1, variation 2, and variation 3. It's a constant process of variation in a certain direction. I think of the Diabelli Variations always myself. And that's very, very free, and varying them very far. I think Brahms's Fourth Symphony, Beethoven's Third, and the last movement of his Ninth Symphony, have variations. Of course, in my second string quartet I have variations, but it's always variations of the same general setup, the general shape of the theme.

Wagner said that Beethoven's Seventh Symphony was the apotheosis of the dance. Berlioz said it was another *Pastoral* Symphony. D'Indy said it was another *Eroica*. Now what do you make out of that? It doesn't change the Seventh Symphony.

You've referred to your Sixth, Seventh, and Eighth Symphonies as constituting some kind of trilogy.

My Sixth, Seventh, and Eighth Symphonies form in my mind a kind of series connected with events of that time. The Sixth Symphony becomes grim at the end, and the Seventh is grim all the way through. The beginning of the Eighth is funereal, and the end is sort of questioning, but lively.

I was very preoccupied by the state of the world at that time. There's a little volume that's just come out about Dallapiccola, and it quotes letters from a lot of other musicians to him. And they quote a letter of mine—it's in Italian, of course. It's true I wanted to write to him, but I was so horrified and ashamed of the war in Vietnam that I put it off. And then I saw him; he was in Ann Arbor for the performance of the Seventh Symphony. I've been told he was always very fond of that piece. But by the Eighth Symphony I'd gotten used to the situation. Of course, an awful lot of things happened in 1968, too. I mean Martin Luther King and Bobby Kennedy were assassinated. There was a little interval when I was more resigned.

The Sixth Symphony was played incomplete the first year. It wasn't finished then. This was in January; then in November the whole thing was played, but it was equally unrecognizable both times. Really unrecognizable.

But I had very good premieres with all the others. The First Symphony, the premiere wasn't so good. The Second Symphony, the premiere was excellent. And when Mitropoulos played it in New York, it was excellent, too. The Third Symphony premiere was bad. I had a wonderful performance by the Chicago Orchestra later. And then the record is—oh, fair. I wouldn't say anything else. The Fourth Symphony, the premiere was very good. It was in Minneapolis. The Fifth Symphony, the premiere was good. The Sixth Symphony, the premiere was a total loss. The Seventh Symphony, the premiere was *excellent*. The Eighth Symphony, the premiere wasn't so good. It wasn't *bad,* but there weren't enough rehearsals by the New York Philharmonic.

> *These pages from the first movement of your Ninth Symphony, which you lent me, look completely ready for performance. Everything's been orchestrated and carefully notated. [See the reproduction of a page of the score on page 180.] But you say that the other movements are not started yet. I'm reminded of a writer who said he always polished each sentence as he went along before he went to the next sentence.*

Yes. Of course, there's much more in this than a sentence of prose. I mean, that's in a way a one-dimensional, superficial way. I understand that Flaubert used to shout his sentences out loud before he considered them finished. And he worked very, very hard. But that's a little different, because when one makes a sketch one sketches a line and one doesn't work out all the details. At least that's the way I do it.

> *You said this is a different method of work from the way you've been composing prior to this piece. I had the feeling that in some pieces various movements could have been worked on in different order at different times, maybe leaving one and going to another and then coming back. Whereas this one seems very systematic, starting at the beginning and getting everything just right and then going on.*

Well, one knows what's going to be over there, but you've got to get there.

And you feel it's essential to have all the orchestration worked out before you get to the end of this movement?

No, not necessarily. But if you get that far, you might just as well finish it up. If you have a real sense of the whole. I mean this is the way I compose now. Forty years ago, when I wrote my Violin Concerto, and for *Montezuma,* too, I wrote a particell out before I did this. I think this is just the way it is at this point. Also, you *do* have to think of the instruments and what they can do.

When these ideas came to you in sketch form, did they appear just as a line, or with the instrumentation?

You generally know what the instruments are going to be, the main instruments. But of course, they have to be supported by other instruments. If you're writing a passage for four horns, you've got to be careful you don't get out of the range. Maybe this seems rather vague. You don't really think it out. You just hear it and put down what you hear.

So, for instance, the rest of this movement that's been sketched ahead is sketched in a particell form with the basic instrumentation?

Yes, but not connected. I mean there are certain things that you can wait till the last moment for. A lot of the writing for percussion, for example. I've known there's got to be something there, but just which instruments you use where, one doesn't bother with that at the beginning. And then there are doublings. Here you've got the cello and the doublebass in unison and the bassoon and the contrabassoon. At just what point should I bring in the bass clarinet there? Of course, I had to drop the contrabassoon, because these notes up here in measure 114 don't sound well on it. They'd be somewhat difficult anyway.

So the main ideas are originally conceived as the lines, and also for specific instruments, and then the other things—transitions between ideas and the filling out of accompaniment to those main ideas—all come later?

You can have a main line. The line that carries things ahead is not always the principal idea. The principal ideas may be underneath it. I have books of sketches from my early years. Some of them are worthless. The books have become much smaller now. Now I have these little books. All sorts of stuff in there that I've put down, and some of it is worthwhile, some of it isn't. I don't date these things—life is too short.

There is a pitfall with this. When one knows one's done one's best, one has to know it and not keep tinkering with it just in the fear that one hasn't.

All my waste paper is in the Princeton Library, or it will be, eventually. The only trouble with anyone ordering my sketches is that I make my sketches on separate sheets of paper and sometimes I go back and refer to them and I don't put the paper back where it belongs. So I couldn't possibly tell you, even for what I'm writing at the time, what order the sketches should be in. Because they're often just little memoranda. I'm a very disorderly man. Just start my wife talking about that sometime.

43

I've tried to keep these things in classified order. One folder says of "Current relevance," the other folder says of "Present relevance." "Current" comes before "Present." "Present" is what I'm thinking about ahead; "Current" is the details of what I'm working on at the moment. I couldn't possibly tell you how these things come. And some of them are just there for reference, probably unnecessary reference.

It would be of interest to find out how much sketch material there is, even if it's not in order, for each given work.

I think it's all there. Except way back I think I threw a lot of this stuff away, and then somebody scolded me for throwing so much of it away, so I didn't throw it any more.

Some composers sketch a great deal for a relatively little amount of music, and other composers do very little sketching.

You keep an awful lot in your head and don't bother to put it down. That's in a way the most important part. Because all the indications of where you're going are in here [pointing to his head] and there's no way of putting them down on paper.

Probably all my sketches through 1972 are in the Princeton Library. The only thing is that I used to get tax deductions for donating them, and then suddenly they stopped. Congress voted that there could only be tax deductions for paper and pencils, which doesn't amount to very much. I think this must have been because our late, unlamented President Nixon got into trouble over that. Because he fell afoul of the date April 1972. So the Internal Revenue Service backdated all this material, and a lot of people are getting into trouble over that, too. That was one of the articles that he would have been impeached on. So my wife and I thought it's much better to leave them to my children.

I found the night before last, I was reading over the whole [ninth] symphony. I'd just put it out of my mind for a month, so I thought I'd read it through and see whether I think it's any good or not. The results were very gratifying on the whole. I suddenly came on a passage in the last movement, I thought, "My God, did I *really* intend to write this?" Because there was a violin part which seemed to stop in the middle and not finish and there was an abrupt change to a passage in the woodwinds. So I looked at my sketches and I found that when I started a new page, I was so busy bringing the woodwinds and everything that I forgot all about the two last notes of the violin line.

I've used the glockenspiel before the Ninth Symphony. I don't like it so much, but I've used it. The glockenspiel and the vibraphone make a high treble and alto combination as the marimba and the xylophone do. If a row is symmetrical [combinatorial], you start with the last note of the second row and end on the first note of the first row. You go backward, but you rearrange the notes in each hexachord. Here's the row of the Seventh Symphony. This is why it's symmetrical, because I can get the inversion of that with these notes.[4]

In the cantata I didn't discover this until I was well along in the piece.

The all-interval business doesn't make any difference at all as far as the actual use of the material is concerned. Only if you use the row absolutely rigidly does the all-interval row make any difference. In fact, I'm not sure it does, because I've never used it that rigidly and nobody ever has, except some of the hard-liners, so to speak.

Take one of the two rows in my Ninth Symphony. The other one is just a row, which is perfectly good, too. A B♭ E♭ F D C♯; G♯ B G F♯ C E. Now, if I take these notes and arrange them in order A B♭ C♯ D E♭ F and under that C B G♯ G F♯ E—a semitone, then a minor third, two more semitones, then a whole tone. Here's the same thing going in the other direction.

Do you consciously exploit the resulting vertical intervals as an entity?

No, not necessarily. It's what I can get out of this. You can use these as harmonies, as Schoenberg does in his fourth quartet, for instance, or use these hexachords as harmonies while this is going on. I mean if you were going to use the row simultaneously—make harmonies out of the hexachords—then the order of the notes becomes really subordinate, because that harmonic combination can give you all sorts of other forms. And very often it's a point of what notes you have available, because the main thing is that you don't have awkward repetitions of these notes. For instance, in my Ninth Symphony now there's a place where both these rows develop—this row and the other one I'm using, which is in a sense a variant of this row, but it's not symmetrical any more. It's a free row, but it plays a role. So I have this row and the other row. The other row forms a framework against which this row plays.

At what point does a thing like this symmetrical row and the musical imagination begin working? That's the point. I found myself the other day making a sketch and I was concentrating on one part of the row and with it I was having another voice. I found what I really was doing was another form. And that was much better.

Is that how you came upon the second row for the Ninth Symphony, or did you start out with two rows?

No, these were both independent ideas. To tell the truth, the first four notes were what I started with. And then these notes come in very slowly at first, then they work up. The oboe and the muted trumpet start with the first two notes, and then horns come in with the second two notes, and then, bang, the rest of the notes come in. The other row comes in about eight measures later. It's a rather explosive idea which I use in varying forms at special moments, because the movement goes on, especially in the last section. That plays a greater part. And various forms of it are used more and more there.

So it overpowers the first row?

Well, they both win out in the end.

Is this the first piece you've written with two different rows operating at the same time?

In a way. But I varied them so much in the Seventh Symphony. I combine these. And I guess in the Sixth Symphony, too. I do what the spirit moves, provided it goes in the piece where it belongs. I found that there was a relationship between the two rows.

Well, that will satisfy future analysts, at any rate.

Yes. But all I would demand of future analysts, and unfortunately that isn't always met with, that the principles are here [pointing to his heart] and not here [pointing to his head].

2

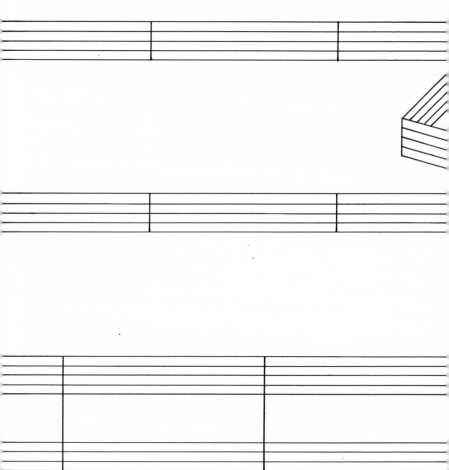

Instrumental

Music

The Three Chorale Preludes for Organ are the first works I wrote after *The Black Maskers*. *The Black Maskers* was a very important work for me, because it was the first big work I wrote after I studied with Bloch, after I felt I really could do what I wanted, which is always a relative thing. I mean you have to learn to do *what* you want sometimes. I felt I was a full-fledged composer.

Now, I had really gotten to know thoroughly some of the big works of Stravinsky shortly before that. I had been acquainted with them before, but I didn't really feel that I knew them, because the orchestral scores weren't published. I played the *Sacre du Printemps* four hands, and I *thought* that I knew what it was like, but the four-hand arrangement is an awfully funny affair. It must be something that Stravinsky slung together, or somebody slung together for rehearsals of the ballet in Paris. I got this orchestral score, and I was absolutely bowled over by it. For four days I literally thought of nothing else—I got all that score into my mind. I was very taken. I knew other works of Stravinsky. I knew *Les Noces,* for instance. There were things that worried me—not worried me, I accepted it for what it was, but I knew that I wanted to do something different.

In writing *The Black Maskers* I felt that there were certain things that I would have liked to do but I simply hadn't learned *how* to do yet, especially in harmonic terms. I could think of what, in those days, were "complex" harmonies. In the first movement of *The Black Maskers* they occur. But I found it very hard to move them in the way I wanted. That was the main thing. I wanted to *not* write works like the Stravinsky works, where the harmonies were in blocks. They don't flow exactly, but they shift. That was the way it seemed to me at the time.

When I look back on it, I find that I knew more than I thought I did. I wanted to develop along those lines. But the point was that I wanted to gain more fluidity and a stronger emphasis on line. I felt now that the line was there in *The Black Maskers* in spite of myself, almost. But that wasn't what I was interested in. I was interested in colors and the harmonies, sort of a psychological complexity.

I was in Florence in August 1924. It was very hot. I said to myself, "I won't try to compose this summer; I'll just go around, case the joint, so to speak." I was in Paris first, then in London, spent a month with some very dear friends of mine outside of Geneva, and down to Florence. I was going down to Rome for a few weeks. I found that I didn't have so much money left as I thought I had, and furthermore I was so in love with Florence that I decided to spend a month there instead of going down to Rome. I was all alone. I spoke very little Italian then. I took a siesta every day. One day I found myself writing. I wrote this first chorale there. And I realized that these were the lines along which I wanted to go and to get that kind of mobility that I wanted in my music.

I learned the direction in which I would gain that kind of fluency. It was a question of not only harmonies specifically, but the whole movement. What I really did was to go into more of an emphasis on line and less on color. As a matter of fact, that has *always* been my musical nature. When my father took my music to Humperdinck and Puccini, what the musicians remarked on was the continuity always. So, in a sense, that's my bent.

When I was younger, I hadn't studied a thing, and I didn't know what to study, and if anybody told me I ought to study harmony, I was furious. And quite mistaken, of course. The way harmony was taught at that time—in a way, my instincts were in the right direction. Because it was very dry. Even when I first went to Bloch, I didn't see the sense in all that I had studied, and he showed me that studying harmony in the right way *did* make sense. Counterpoint, too, especially.

Do you have any extra-musical associations with the second chorale?

That's rather interesting, because I was in Paris that summer. I was really quite unhappy, upset for various reasons. I lived in a place on the Boulevard Montparnasse where my window overlooked the gardens of a convent. And there was a bell that tolled every quarter of an hour. And when I wrote this I realized this A$^\sharp$ was that bell. Later on, when I wrote the last movement of my first piano sonata—that really is in the key of D-sharp minor, although the signature is C-sharp major. (I thought it *was* in C-sharp major for a while, but then I realized that it was really modal in D-sharp minor. A sort of Dorian mode.) Naturally, I'd thought of the ending long before I'd finished a lot of the rest. The ending was a D-sharp minor ending. There's one little moment in it where there's this upper line around A$^\sharp$. When I finished, I thought, "My God, that A$^\sharp$ just rings out all the time. Maybe by subconscious association." I thought, "A$^\sharp$ means something very poignant to me." I thought, "I'll just have to look this over tomorrow morning." I had it all copied out. My wife and I and friends went out to dinner that night. I slept well. The next morning I looked the sonata over, and A$^\sharp$ was all gone. A$^\sharp$ was there naturally, but there was no more association. It had kept running in my ear like a kind of knell, you know. I suppose momentarily I was taken back to this very dark mood.

Would you not commit yourself to a key for the second chorale?

I would dodge the issue of what key it's in. But it is certainly written from a tonal point of departure. It certainly goes to F-sharp major here at measure 15 and ends on the dominant of G-sharp minor.

No. 3 is in E-flat major. That one goes well on the organ all right, but I was a little disappointed when I first heard it, because I wanted a kind of accent that you can't get on the organ. I forgot completely that you couldn't get it. The organ is not my instrument. I'd like the first two bars to be on trombones, although it would be very difficult for them. That's the only way I worked out of notating it. All these rhythms I wanted to have more sharply brought out than the organ can do, that's all. But it goes perfectly well.

I don't like the term "relative minor," because it's really another key. E-flat minor would be the same key as E-flat major. The relative minor just happens to have the same key signature, that's all. The borderline between tonality and atonality is a very, very wide one. You don't step over the threshold from one into another. You have to go down a long, long, long corridor.

Generally speaking, then, the first and third pieces are nearer the beginning of the corridor, and the second piece is a little farther along.

Maybe, maybe. I think they all are on the way. I considered my Second Symphony essentially tonal, but nobody else did. I was asked by a lot of people why I wrote key signatures. Darius Milhaud asked of my opera *The Trial of Lucullus,* "Why did you put key signatures in it?" And I said, "Of course, I made my sketches without putting accidentals in and I thought of them in terms of key signatures. And I was too lazy to put in all those accidentals." And he said, "It's funny. I leave the key signatures out, because I'm too lazy to put them in."

But everybody else thought my Second Symphony was atonal. Of course, I don't approve of that term. Schoenberg disapproved of it for the same reason, although for years I thought he was mistaken. It's a sort of mechanical and conventional differentiation. Naturally, between Schoenberg and Haydn, or between Webern and Haydn, or Boulez and Haydn, or between me and Haydn there's a great difference. Obviously. And one doesn't think in terms of key relationships at all. But there are always relationships between notes, and that's why the term "atonal" is wrong. It depends on a very rigid definition of tonality, which nobody, really, has ever made or accepted. But if somebody says that a piece is *not* based on contrasts between keys, it makes a lot of sense.

> *By writing the Three Chorale Preludes for Organ did you feel that you mastered a certain vocabulary of harmonies?*

I would say that I became conscious of possibilities that I achieved later. When I wrote this, I was writing a *piece,* of course, I wasn't doing an exercise. I didn't naturally foresee the outcome of it, because if I'd known that, I'd have written my Eighth Symphony, my cantata, my Double Concerto, all my latest works *then*. But I couldn't have. It took years to. Just the gradual evolution of my style, I suppose. I don't consider that I've made any abrupt changes; it's been a steady evolution. Even when I wrote in the twelve-tone system finally, it was almost against my will. It wasn't *against* my will, but it was not conscious: I sort of slipped into it, so to speak. Even *that* was a gradual development. I had accepted Schoenberg's twelve-tone music long before I accepted the system in any real sense.

> *You wrote about the genesis of the first piano sonata in* The Musical Experience.[1] *You also mentioned when we discussed the* Three Chorale Preludes *that the Sonata is in a sort of modal D-sharp. It ends on a D♯, of course. But it begins in B minor.*

I feel that the D♯ is a note which one remembers from the beginning. The D♯, E♭ there. I haven't looked at this for years.

I was walking around the streets of Pisa after having dropped my sister-in-law off at the train station and this harmony came into my mind [at number 235] and I got intrigued. I kept working it out in my mind. And I thought, "This is a piano sonata." My sister-in-law was studying the piano. I said I'd write her a piece. Of course, I didn't realize that she couldn't possibly play a piece like that, but I didn't know that at the time.

And the next day I went home to Florence, and I got this theme of the Allegro. Now I was going to start with that. I began thinking about it and working about it, and then shortly after that, I was in Vienna, and I did some more. I've forgotten just what passages occurred to me. I think maybe this whole Allegro section. Then I played it. I never could make this sound right. Then I suddenly realized that the reason was that it starts out with a syncopation, and since there's no beat established, the syncopation can't come off.

So immediately I thought that I'd write a slow introduction and establish that beat. So this is the result. The melody came to my mind at the same time, and the key. (Here's the D$^\sharp$ again at measure 24.) Then, of course, I got the ideas for the other movements.

I knew that this was not really an introduction, that it was the exposition of the slow movement, and so the slow movement is interrupted by the whole first movement. Then I thought of this theme [molto vivace], the beginning of the last movement. When I got there I thought, "It mustn't begin on a C$^\sharp$, it must go one tone higher." First I thought it would be C-sharp major, but the C-sharp major never seemed to come, so it was obvious that the principal harmony was the D-sharp major. That's essentially what happened. The life and adventures of D-sharp. [laughter]

> Not to mention the life and adventures of the A$^\sharp$, which you mentioned was the knell.

Oh yes. That was just sort of an obsession. Here's the A$^\sharp$ at number 510, you see. This A$^\sharp$ just haunted me. I wrote this whole last page in one afternoon, and I was awfully tired. There were other things involved, too. I originally wanted to have this played at the first of the Copland–Sessions concerts. And I engaged myself to write it. Well, I didn't have nearly enough time. I thought

I could write it very quickly. I was traveling around in the meantime. This was started in the fall of 1927 and then I moved back to the United States. And I really got going on it in the United States in the spring.

I suddenly had to face the fact that I couldn't possibly finish even the first movement in time. So I decided I was going to give them it so they could play these two movements. I sat up one night and just finished that first movement. The second movement was okay. It was this whole section [on pages six and seven of the Schott score] that was a problem. I decided I'd write them something that could be played, and it was played, but I knew I was going to work it out later. And I *never* would do that again in my life.[2] Well, it wouldn't happen to me later at all. I had always worked very well under pressure but the pressure was too heavy and the time was too short, that's all. That's a trauma, an experience like that.

I remember this part [number 120 on] took me a long time, and I worked hard and I got obsessed and made dozens of sketches. I knew what I wanted, I knew what key I wanted and everything. There was a young man by the name of Alberto Moravia. We went to walk one day, and I told him what was going on. I said, "I have to find a way to continue the piece I'm writing now. And I could describe to you in detail what I want—what's got to be there—but I haven't got the notes."

One day I said, "This has got to stop. I'm obsessed by this and getting nowhere, so I've got to get my mind off this." I was living outside of Florence and went down and took the streetcar and went to the movies. As I came out of the movie, there was the theme in my mind. The right theme. That's the way things happen sometimes. And that same sort of thing has happened to me again but without any of the agony and the torture.

In my Harvard lectures I talked about this, because

this is quite a well-known process to people who are creative in any field. I refer to an extremely interesting book by a French mathematician called *The Psychology of Invention in the Mathematical Field*.[3] He starts out by quoting a letter by Mozart—it's ascribed to Mozart, it's never been verified that he wrote it because there's no copy of it in his handwriting, but it was reported by a friend of his. If he didn't write it, I'd like to hear some music by the composer who *did* write it, because it describes so well, naturally in Mozart's own terms, what forming a conception of a piece is like. People have been astonished, because he says, "I think of it, and gradually I see the whole thing at once, in a sort of simultaneous vision." Well, I know what he means by that. He says, "Of course, not in detail. That's to be worked out later."

When you think of somebody you know, you can suddenly see him, but you aren't conscious of the detail—you can't describe his eyes or his nose. You have to work on that and identify everything. Or if you hear somebody's voice, you recognize it immediately without being able to describe it. Or if I think of, let's say the *Eroica* Symphony, I see the whole *Eroica* there, but I have to sort of go through it. There's a synthetic picture that comes to one's mind.

People have wondered how Mozart could say he could see the whole composition at a glance. Well, when I wrote about it, I said there was really nothing so extraordinary, because if I think of Andrea Olmstead, I have a kind of image. And I can fill it out. Well, she wears her hair in this way. Then I think her nose is like this and her mouth is like that. And I think of not only what you look like, but what you talk like, the way you move and everything else. I don't have to think of a person. I can think of a piece of music. If I think of *Tristan and*

Isolde, I immediately can reconstruct the whole score more or less from that.

The first four notes of the *Eroica* begin a little overture of an opera Mozart wrote when he was thirteen years old. People say that's a great theme, but what makes it great is what Beethoven did out of it. One has a clear idea of the character of a piece. It doesn't mean that you will know exactly how the first movement will end. But you have a very limited choice.

In other words, it's the foreknowledge of what the whole will be like that allows you to be specific at any given point?

Yes.

I got the theme, and from then on, I won't say it was entirely smooth sailing, because once you've done a thing like that, then you are tense about every moment, and you have to have it take shape. Now, this passage at measures 140–50 was the worst, because I knew this [the ottava section] was coming in. And I worked, and worked, and worked, and finally I thought to myself, "Well, this goes, but it isn't really what I'd like to write." A little while afterwards I looked at it and said to myself, "It's just right, of course." I was being so hypercritical that until it moved naturally, it was torture. It was just that the experience of writing this whole thing was much the toughest time I've ever had as a composer.

You call the first movement of your first string quartet a "three-stanza form."

It's a little like the A-minor quartet of Beethoven, which is really three expositions instead of an exposition, development, and recapitulation. And each exposition is a variation of the one before it in a certain sense. More in this than in Beethoven; in Beethoven they're more similar. Even the Beethoven quartet is sometimes described as the usual sonata form, but ignoring the whole tonal structure of the work. The third exposition is sometimes called the "coda." That's a lot of sheer nonsense.

This quartet has the same idea; this first theme is always varied each time. The center of gravity is different in both of them. The last movement is probably the most orthodox movement I ever wrote. But it's a lot of fun. To me it brings back the smell of sagebrush and the lovely place out in the country where I lived in Nevada. I rode horseback.

I heard it a few years ago after a long time. It had become easy. "They played it the way they'd play a quartet by Haydn," I said afterwards. It was recorded by the Galimir Quartet. The only trouble is, they thought at the studio it would be a nice thing if I took over the controls. It was a very nice idea, but I didn't do it very well. It was a very good performance, but I sort of wrecked the record, I'm afraid.

This quartet was played four times, by four different quartets. Each quartet, although the quartets themselves were very different in quality, played it a little better from the musical standpoint. They understood it a little better. I've never been able to explain that. Some people to whom I've explained it understood very well. But one man, a second violinist, said, "That's sheer nonsense." I said, "But it happened." None of them had heard the other quartet play it, but just the fact that it had been played somehow made it sit more easily. I think because the style is better understood.

The only time I had a first-class performance at the very beginning was when the Pro Art Quartet played my second quartet. Rudolf Kolisch was one of the greatest performers I have ever known. Certainly one of the greatest chamber music players. I told him once, "This is the only time I had a work played at the first performance the way it would normally take fifteen years to get a performance like that." He was terribly pleased. But it's true.

I took the three "stanzas," as you called them, of the first movement of String Quartet No. 1 and then compared the first theme, the second theme, and the closing theme of each of these three stanzas.

This theme [measure 75] is the same one. And the third time it comes in on the cello [measure 168]. You have it on the violin first [measure 75], and then the next time on the viola over here [measure 79], and then the third time on the cello. And then answered by the viola [measure 170]. And then this comes in a closer imitation. All the way through you have a kind of stretto. I would say this is the closing theme [measure 224]. In each exposition you have the same order in which the things appear, but they're always a little different.

Would you call this at measure 224 a coda?

Yes, but of course the second movement is supposed to come in without any pause.

So in a way it's an introduction to the second movement?

Well, it's a transition, I suppose. The third stanza begins in the cello [measure 168].

About some of the key schemes involved here: We start off in E minor, even though it seems to be E-flat major, and then this modulates to C minor for the second theme.

Yes, but of course, even here it isn't to a key you modulate so much as to a harmony. The harmony may be the dominant. That's quite true, the signature is right, but where is the tonic? Certainly it's the key of C minor, but it never comes to a cadence. This really begins a kind of phase—well maybe it had begun with my Violin Concerto—in my work where I was getting away from the cadence very much. But I wasn't away from tonal structure yet.

Could you explain this chord at measure 28?

I would say it was in the key of G minor. But it's only a sort of passing inflection in the direction of G minor. There's no outspoken G minor, simply this [measure 25 on] is like a kind of dominant. Measure 27 is the nearest to a tonic it ever gets in G minor, but it quickly goes back to E minor [measure 29].

The first theme is implied here [measure 79], whereas the closing theme is implied directly above it.

The transition is not a real statement of the theme. It begins like the first theme and goes along. But the theme itself always changes. Even in my Second Symphony I used key signatures. I was asked over and over again why I used them. I've seen the Second Symphony referred to as a "symphony in D minor." That's the way I thought of it, but the D minor is very well hidden. Not purposely; I was thinking of D minor as a reference, undoubtedly. It's not a twelve-tone piece, or anything like that.

This *is* a sort of a D-minor cadence at the very end of the quartet, but again it's a somewhat tenuous one. From measure 89 on I would say was perhaps E-flat minor.

At one time I felt that there was a relation between the key system and the contour of that melodic line itself. I can't quite see that now. I'd have to go over the quartet to find it. But I don't think that was intentional. I think I discovered it afterwards.

At measure 25 I thought I heard a slight reference to Schoenberg's Verklärte Nacht.

I would doubt it very much, because I don't think I'd ever heard it at that time. I didn't hear it till years later. As a matter of fact, when I did hear it first, it was on a string orchestra, and I think it's really much more beautiful than the sextet. I wouldn't mind . . . [laughter]

Regarding the second movement, Edward T. Cone points out in his article[4] the motivic similarity of the first three notes in the first violin part to other parts of the movement.

Oh yes, that keeps coming in all the time, fragmentarily. It's even there [measure 282]. I wasn't aware of it at the time, but I think after I'd written it I was aware of it, because it comes in and is made very explicit. It's even in inversion here [measure 281].

Could you describe the form of this as an adagio, a trio or scherzo, and back to the adagio?

There's a very short interlude; it's like a scherzo episode.

The key for the scherzo eludes me.

I think it's E minor, isn't it? But it goes from one key to another. It comes back to this theme [at measure 377]. The E minor is again very tenuous; it's just a sort of locality. I wouldn't know what key we're in there [at measure 320]. One would have to take it note by note.

In other words, this section of the whole quartet is probably the most elusive as far as pinning down a tonality is concerned. I take it you probably wanted a contrast between a fairly stable area and a less stable area?

Oh, yes, absolutely.

And then when we get back to the adagio, we're back in B minor. However, your accompaniment differs; it's not a strict repetition.

Yes, exactly. There's this counter-rhythm in pizzicato. And then [measure 408] there's a canon with the second violin and a secondary figure here [viola measure 409]. And this [measure 430] develops differently again and comes down. I remember I was writing this section [measure 439 on], and not knowing quite what I was going to do, and this [measures 441–42] came to me. The viola takes over here [measure 449] for a moment, and the line comes back to the second violin [measure 451 g–f♯ eighth notes] and goes way, way up into the sky.

Here [measure 457 viola double stop] is something that is quite unplayable, because both these notes are on the C string. I didn't discover it until later. I remember Alfred Einstein was with me once when we were going to hear this, and he had the score. I told him I was ashamed of this one thing, and he said, "Oh, don't worry about that. Mozart did that once, too." The low D in the double stop is quite unnecessary, because it's right here on the cello.

The way I analyzed the third movement was as a fairly strict sonata-allegro form.

Very strict sonata. The only really regular sonata-allegro I ever wrote. It's an introductory passage, but it's always part of the first theme. The second theme is in the cello. Here's the second theme over here [measure 555]. This [top of page 28] is the closing theme, if you like. It's not really the closing theme; it's the beginning of the last section. When you come to the tonic, or to the dominant, then you can talk about a closing theme. And here [measure 629] begins the development section.

I tell you, I never think of form in those terms at all, because even with the classics there's such a tremendous variety. Every Beethoven symphony is unique; every Beethoven sonata is unique.

The score of your Pages from a Diary *is labeled* From My Diary.

Pages from a Diary—that's my title. There was a man who recorded one of them when I was living in California; he was in New York. And he always called it *From My Diary.* I hate that title. My publisher begged me to let him publish them under that, because the labels for the records were already printed. And I gave in too easily. It's awful. My wife and I were at a concert once where they were played, and there was a friend of ours sitting behind us who didn't like contemporary music. And my wife heard her say to the woman she was sitting with, "That must have been a bad day." The pieces don't mean anything like what the title suggests. I considered calling them *Albumblätter.* I didn't like "album leaves," and I called them *Pages from a Diary* instead. I wrote each one in a day.

When I first wrote the third piece, I didn't have this middle voice. I added that afterwards. It seemed to me that the middle voice was necessary. I was out in Colorado and I had a student, Carter Harman, to whom it's dedicated, actually. He had a new girlfriend—he was a very attractive boy—and he wanted me to meet her. And he was late. We were waiting for him, and he was twenty minutes late. And while we were waiting for him, I sat down and wrote that piece. And afterwards I thought, "The texture is too thin, and it needs a little more movement besides the contrast between these two voices." So I added the middle voice.

I used to keep lots of sketches, I still do, and then I would go through them every now and then. And this first piece is one I'd more or less rejected and given up. When I went back, I thought, "Why did I reject that?" I wanted to make a piece out of it.

The story about number four is that I wanted to write another piece to go with the others; this was written later. They all were written very quickly. I like to put the dates at the end. But this shows that it's not "from my diary."

They were not originally intended to be combined?

No.

But they do *seem to work together.*

Yes, of course. I'm writing these little piano pieces now [Five Pieces for Piano]. But when you make a series of them, you put them in a certain order. For instance, I've written three, and I'm now on the fourth, and there's going to be a fifth. The first three go in the order in which they were written. The one I'm doing now is going to be number five, and there's going to be another in between, because I want the order slow–fast–moderate–fast–slow, that's all.

The one that interested me the most is the fourth in this set. I conceive of it in two-bar groups, which I simply

called "A" and "B." The chordal idea is "A" and the
melodic idea is "B."

Yes. It's a sort of pompous idea and a little sort of
scherzando idea at the same time. This is sort of paro-
distic, this movement. It's a dialogue between something
rather weighty and something slightly mocking.

Do you find, as a pianist, that writing for the piano is
somehow "easier" or more approachable than for any
other instrument?

No, I would say I think in orchestral terms most easily.
Even though it's piano music. I don't really have much
difficulty in that way, I wouldn't say at all. When I say
"orchestral"—my music is essentially polyphonic and I
think of it very much in terms of color. *Pages from a Dairy*
is conceived very much in terms of colors. And my new
piano pieces here are thought of in terms of color.

By "color" you mean both registral color and . . .

Yes, and then the color of the way the chords are
grouped. I mean you have this very simple third down
here, a major ninth here, and then a seventh up there,
and this interval here. And then the color of the particular figures that are used. I mean, this is as much color as
anything else.

I brought in the New Music Edition of your Duo for Violin and Piano.

This is a very bad edition, a sort of amateurish job, that's all. It was republished fifteen years ago by Marks. They took over all my earlier works. Everything except my Second Symphony, which Schirmer wouldn't sell them. They republished my Violin Concerto, and they republished this.

I called it a duo because I was tired of calling things sonatas, although it is a sonata. And I found English words. I'm so used to the Italian words, which sort of required a regular conventional meaning, and I felt they were more precise.

In your discussion of the piece on the record jacket[5] you describe the four formal divisions of the piece.

Let me read it. [laughter] I always feel like a fool when I write these things, I assure you. This piece is really in a way like the form of my first piano sonata. [reading the liner notes] It's a blow-by-blow description; it's all you can do. "Fast, gay, with fire"—the word "gay" had a different meaning in those days. I was much more conscientious about program notes then than I am now, because I think they're for the birds.

You have some ideas of your own about the sonata-allegro form.

I think essentially this: that the sonata-allegro form was never defined until some twenty years after Beethoven's death. And that it was something which evolved, it wasn't invented out of a hat. It was originally the result of the fact that composers had, because of equal temperament, all the keys at their disposal. They had the whole gamut of major and minor keys, and they could modulate wherever they wanted. This led to a broader extension simply of musical design. It brought about the possibility of sharper contrasts. The problem was how to build a piece and have very important contrasts in it. Eventually a kind of hierarchy of contrasts based on key relationships and key centers was built up.

Composers were enormously inventive in finding ways to solve that problem. As a result, no two Haydn quartets—of which there are eighty-six, I believe—are alike. (I read all of them through once when I had a nasty penicillin reaction. I was in bed absolutely miserable for a week, and the only thing that kept me going was just reading through them from no. 1 to opus 77, no. 2. Maybe there are more of them now, I don't know.[6]) The amazing thing is that I felt that they were all different— great invention. There were no rules.

And I find the same thing in Mozart. I found the same thing in Beethoven, and to a certain extent I found the same thing in Schubert, although Schubert died when he was thirty-one years old, which is quite young after all. He'd have been Beethoven's equal, if he'd lived. In a certain way he was, almost.

Then after the principles and rules were laid down, there was a certain sameness in design in all big works for a while. This is why in Schumann, Chopin, and certainly Liszt, and even Brahms early in his life, the form becomes simply a kind of mold in which you pour the music.

I shocked my students once by saying that as far as

the general setup is concerned, there's much more similarity between a symphony by Tchaikovsky and a symphony by Brahms than there is between one Beethoven symphony and another. Brahms is more closely knit and more tightly constructed, but you always have your first theme of a certain length, you have a transition period, which sometimes in the classics is practically no transition period, just a sharp contrast, which is very effective, too. And you have a second theme; then the design of the second section of the second theme is the same— there are several ideas, sort of a lyrical idea at the beginning and then a more dramatic one, and then a closing theme. And then the development sections always follow a similar pattern. In other words, the thing had become sort of standardized. Now we don't feel obliged to end in the same key as we begin in, provided the movements follow each other logically. It's very hard to define that logic sometimes.

Atonality implied that there's no relation between the notes at all, and that's not true. No more true in Schoenberg than it was in Bach or Haydn. But what it is, is no tonal center can be unequivocally defined, that's all. Now, what I found as I went along is that you have to give up sustaining tonal contrasts, because the character of the harmonies doesn't allow that kind of sustained contrast. You can give the feeling, and sometimes I want to, momentarily, of a very sharp tonal contrast. But it isn't even a contrast between a key and another; it's a contrast between a chord and another, really. The influence of that chord is very clear at the moment, but it can't be kept up because anything but a triad or a very simple seventh chord can go in all sorts of directions. And it doesn't imply one direction, except in a very specific tonal context.

I had felt that the first and third movements were more ambiguous tonally than the second and fourth movements. You provide key signatures for the second and fourth movements but not for the first and third.

Well, the first and third are the same essentially. The third movement is a development; it has that second contrast.

It does end in G major.

The last movement is really in G major. But it's in a sort of region of one sharp. I like this ending very much. It's very, very nice, I think. I think this piece was quite important in developing my harmonic style. It's more chromatic than my first quartet.

It's very hard sometimes to say when one actually began a piece. I could say that my second quartet was written between 1937 and 1951. I mean, I just had some of the ideas for it then. Then I worked on the first movement for a long time, and the other movements I wrote quite quickly.

The publisher of the second string quartet insisted on having every movement begin at the beginning of a line. In my manuscript I had them coming in the middle of a line if necessary. So on the record of the New Music Quartet the engineer ruined the record by stopping between movements, which he shouldn't do. It's a strenuous piece, because it should be played without pause.

The principal lines, Hauptstimme, *are indicated for the first time in your music.*

I put those in *after* one performance, when the quartet didn't bring out the voice-leading enough. When you have a complicated polyphonic texture, it's very, very important that the voices be kept in perspective with each other, otherwise they kill each other off.

Also in your notation for this piece the accent marks and glissandi are in parentheses.

The accents indicated the shape of the phrase. But the parenthesis means don't exaggerate it, just feel the phrase properly. I've asked players who've played this quartet if they thought I overmarked my music, and they said, "No, not at all. We always know exactly what you want."

On the record jacket you say that the five movements do not contain motive references to one another. I felt that there were some.

There are. I don't know why I said that. What I mean is that you don't in the second movement find a reference to the main ideas of the first movement. Not specifically, anyway. It is very easy to consider this [the first violin line at the opening of the second movement] a kind of inversion of the theme of the variations with a different accentuation, of course.

There are standard forms in this piece, which exist here to a greater extent than in your other works; variations,

ABA forms, double fugues. Is it possible that the return to this type of form was a consequence of the loosening up of the tonal structure to almost a twelve-tone extent?

I never precluded that, of course. Furthermore, you could find earlier works of mine which are much more closely in these forms. The variations are very free. The thing that is really constant in them is simply the shape of the theme. In the first place, I had planned all of the movements ahead of time. And in fact I had planned two other movements, which were to come at the end. When I actually got to the last movement, I thought, "That's where it really ends." I used the sketches I had for the other movements in later works. Furthermore, five movements played without pause is quite enough.

But I think that I was challenged by not the forms as such, but the tightness and tremendous solidity of construction which they represented. And, as I've told you before, I don't consider the standard forms standard in any way. I think they're just files that you file things away in. Because within those forms there's a tremendous, almost superhuman inventiveness just on the formal level. I was challenged at that time. I didn't feel I was going back to something; I felt I was going forward in my own development. As forms, those forms mean *nothing,* because really masterly construction means everything. The forms themselves can be awful in the wrong hands. And they don't guarantee anything—having a recapitulation in the original key doesn't guarantee anything at all.

I was thinking about how much the content influenced the form. When the content of some of your pieces was more tonal, the form came out of the content. Whereas when you take a "standard form," it is supposed to do certain things, which of course, as you said, doesn't guarantee that it's going to sound good or work; but it has a formula to it that you can stay within. Did the breakdown of tonality into a more even distribution of chromatics precipitate a reaction—this is going to come out sounding funny—to take refuge in something comfortable to make up for the uncomfortable feeling of not having a tonal system any longer?

The way I look at it, it isn't comfortable at all. And it doesn't in itself solve any problems whatever. But, I think that if a piece is going to have any unity, it should be about something. Not about the Vietnam War or something like that, but it should be about something musically. You never find a form used in anywhere near a very literal sense in the quartet. The nearest it would come to it is in the variations. In my First Symphony and the finale of the first quartet the recapitulation has never been a recapitulation in the classic sense of the word. It's a return to the material of the beginning and developing it differently.

The analogy I was thinking of was that of Schoenberg, who's often described as a neo-classicist in a formal regard.

The most nonsensical thing I ever heard. It doesn't mean a thing.

I think what I was trying to get to was the relationship between a chromatic content and the form in which it is embodied. It struck me as curious that in this piece you used what you quoted were standard forms, and that these forms would appear in a piece so near to your adoption of the twelve-tone system.

Well, if you're going to construct something on a large scale, there have got to be associative elements of some kind. Now, these can be very literal. It is a question of the kind, the character, of the association that comes. You've got to know by the end of the piece that you're listening to the same piece that you were listening to at the beginning. And with tonality, of course, this was very, very strong. The recapitulation was the final affirmation of the tonic. That's what it is structurally. The most obvious way to get that is by literal repetition. These things are not that patly solved.

When people call Schoenberg a neo-classicist, the point is he was grappling with large musical design. And if you're going to grapple with this, you've got to face the problems. With some of the music that would be called non-neo-classic by those same people, you don't really have a large design, that's all. A large design has to be very tight, it's got to be something that imposes itself as a large design, and that was the result of it. You don't find recapitulations in Schoenberg either.

For instance, Boulez writes music that is very long. Well, with all admission that he's a very gifted man, I don't ever feel a sense of large design. I feel that it's just very, very long. It doesn't have very clear shape as a whole. And I enjoy listening to it, but after I've heard it, I don't have a feeling of the piece as a whole, and I don't remember it very clearly. And it's not hard to listen to at all. Schoenberg is very hard to listen to, but he does have the associative elements which are very clearly enunci-ated. This is my basic attitude.

There's one thing that I might mention. This quartet has been related to the C-sharp minor quartet of Beethoven. I realized that I was beginning with a kind of a fugue, not a real fugue at all, but it's a quasi-fugal de-sign. I was aware of that, but I wasn't aware of any of the other things. One friend of mine said, "Well, you've got two scherzi." And I said, "In the first place, the second movement isn't a scherzo at all, and I also would say the second movement of the C-sharp minor isn't a scherzo at all." He said, "The third movement is a set of varia-tions." And I said, "That's true." That resemblance never occurred to me at all. Of course, it ends very differently from the C-sharp minor. When this was played first in New York, there was an interview over the radio. This lady said, "This has been likened to the C-sharp minor quartet of Beethoven. How do you feel about that?" I said, "Well, it's all right with me." My wife laughed afterwards, and I thought I should have said, "You might check with Beethoven." [laughter]

Didn't Andor Foldes premiere the second sonata?

Yes, only literally, but not really, because I didn't rec-ognize it when he played it. He didn't really understand it at all.

I like the way Beveridge Webster plays it.

Yes, that's another kettle of fish. That's a very good recording. He played it beautifully.

I think of the third movement as a very nasty movement. What I mean is that I was thinking of everything I
hated and how much I hated it. I hated the Nazis—I
feel there's a little of the German army in this. I feel
there's a sort of mechanical view of things in this. One
of my students, a very bright girl, said, "It's the beast,
but it's the way you fight the beast, too," and I felt that
was very shrewd of her. Because there is this contrast
between the first kind of sonority and the second kind
of sonority, which is very metallic and sharp and crisp
and a little mechanical. Don't take anything I say too
literally; it's just the things that were on my mind.

The first and the third movements are not really in
sonata form at all. They're a general ABA with different
elements in the A and in the B. The B is not entirely
unrelated to the A.

> *Measure 178, as well as the last measure of the piece,
> puzzles me as far as the rhythmic indications. Why did
> you make this a 3/4 measure plus a 1/4 measure rest
> rather than a 4/4 measure with the last beat a rest?*

Because of the rhythm, the feeling. I don't feel a four
rhythm there at all—I feel a three. The fragments of
this long phrase are somewhat foreshortened. The measure rest is a kind of breathing.

> *Has this to do with what we had talked about before
> with regard to your First Symphony—the idea of a
> downbeat being different from an accent? Perhaps a bar
> of rest is different from a rest within a bar.*

Yes, exactly. Do you remember the very end of the first movement of my First Symphony? It's in regular 5/8 time. It would be quite wrong if that measure before the last chord were still 5/8. The chord has to come after four eighths. That's why I changed the bar at that time. It wouldn't be right otherwise. It would be purely mechanical, and it's got to be where the end really is inevitable. Otherwise, it would seem mechanical and would lose the momentum.

> We talked a bit about whether keys are even applicable to this piece. I had the impression that you were thinking in terms of C major.

As a point of departure, all right, yes. On the other hand, whether it's C major or A minor, I wouldn't know, if you see what I mean. The whole principle of tonal structure is very much dissolved by the time this was written, for me certainly. You could say that you could start with tonality, but it ranges very far out, that's all. But a lot of the kind of thinking that led Schoenberg to that formulation was not so systematic in the sense of being a set of rather rigid rules as some of Schoenberg's followers—notably Webern—wanted to make it. For Schoenberg at first in practice it *was,* but that was because he was exploring its possibilities and discovering them. It's implicit in the letter that he wrote to me, which is in his correspondence,[7] that the music is the point of reference, and not the system.

> What do you think of the recording by Robert Helps as a performance of the third sonata?

I thought it was excellent. I like my music to be played *somewhat* rhapsodically. But I thought that was excellent. Now, I'm not saying that ten years hence there might not be a better one. Performances improve with the age of the work. That's a sad thing, but it's true. Bob Helps is a very, very good pianist and knows my music very well.

> *He's recorded the first sonata also. I noticed that there he uses rubato, even though on the first page it specifies, "senza qualsiasi 'rubato.'"*

Yes, of course, there you are! That was written forty-five years ago, forty-six years ago. And at that time I didn't want my music played the way most people played Chopin. At that time, it was still the tail end of the kind of playing in which the two hands never hit the keys at the same time; the left hand was always a little ahead of time. They thought a little more "expression" could be given that way. I don't think Chopin should be played that way. I think Chopin should be played like music and not with a lot of exaggeration and too much rubato.

I must say also, that at that time I was rather chary of markings, because I *didn't* want any exaggeration, and I thought that a really musical pianist would know how to play it anyway. I found that people even avoided doing things if I didn't put them in afterwards, so I mark my music very differently now. I mean there's a place on that first page where certainly there should be a crescendo, or a slight crescendo, or a diminuendo, but I found that if I didn't put that in, people avoided it. They thought, "That's not what he wants." Well, of course I wanted it to be played like music. But I've learned that a lot of people don't really know what music is.

Music should always be shaped. A phrase should have a shape when it's played. The last note and the first note are not the same, and the phrase develops. These are things that a singer would do, but an instrumental player doesn't always do.

I learned also many years ago that it was fatal to bully the performer, let's say to overbully the performer. You just inhibit him if you do that. He's got to play the music as he reacts to it. Now, if there are exaggerations, one can correct them. And if I say the left hand is too loud in a certain place, if I say, "Maybe you could relax a little more at that point" or the opposite, I could help a little. But I learned that the less you bully performers, the better results you get, that's all. And furthermore, one performance is not the only performance there's going to be. I'm always convinced of that. And if it were, then the situation is hopeless anyway. [laughter]

It took a long time to work out the Violin Sonata with a violinist, because I'd written the notes, and he told me they couldn't be played. Several things had to be worked out. I wanted measure 81 to be done very fast. Well, it can't be done very fast!

The whole piece is very difficult technically.

Oh, yes, impossible, quite impossible. I haven't looked at this for years, and I like it. [laughter] But it's absolutely, infernally difficult. In fact, it's difficult as hell.

The first couple of times I listened to the recording, I couldn't think very much about the piece. As a former violinist, I was only thinking about how difficult it was to play.

What recording did you listen to?

Bress.

Oh, yes, that's not good at all. I'm sorry, but it's not good at all. Matthew Raimondi plays it wonderfully. There is a somewhat better recording than the one you heard by the man who first played it, Robert Gross. This is the traditional way to play Bach sonatas, but I don't think Bach should be played that way, but that's not my business exactly. For good or ill, you've got to play it in time. You just can't take your time with a complicated double stop.

As far as the general outline of this last movement goes, I called the section at measure 607 a coda. The second movement was an ABA, and the third a type of rondo.

Well, I never thought of those forms when I was writing the music. I just feel that there are certain basic principles about large-scale design in music. In the first place, the music has got to go ahead. What occurs over here at measure 574 has got to add something to what occurs here at measure 490, even if it's simply a matter of context sometimes. In other words, a recapitulation has got to be at least as interesting as the exposition, in a sense, maybe even more interesting. But it's interesting in a different way. There you're at home and perfectly free to go to town.

Would you call this a recapitulation, beginning here at measure 574?

It's a variation. If you call a thing a "recapitulation" in my music, it's *always* a variation of one kind or another.

Maybe we should find a different terminology for a bringing back of an idea? If we were to invent a term for this reference, chucking "recapitulation" because it has too many connotations of sonata-allegro form and too many tonal connotations . . .

Well, it means that you repeat the first chapter, that's literally what "recapitulation" means. It's a summing up, in a way, although the last part in my music is more than a summing up. It's still a going ahead, adding a little.

But I object to all terminology. Naturally, I'm being silly about it, a little, because I like to recognize things, and without terminology you don't. If I see an animal out there, I want to know whether it's a cat or a dog. If I see somebody going down the street, I like to know whether it's a boy or a girl. That's been rather important in my life. [laughter]

Writing about your music, I am forced to use terminology.

I've read so much stupid stuff that I'm fed up with certain things, that's all. And it's purely emotional, I assure you, in the most trivial sense of the word. I would rather have you talk about "*a* recapitulation," rather than "*the* recapitulation," if you see what I mean. That's all. Furthermore, anybody has a right to say what he wants. If what's said basically hits the point, I'm pleased.

I recall an idea very plainly and specifically without

repeating it literally. I very rarely repeat anything literally, because that doesn't seem to be in the nature of this vocabulary.

In the violin sonata there's an exact da capo.

Yes, just in the second movement. I thought, "Well, what's the use of fussing with this when it comes back, because it moves so fast? And also in the second quartet it's the same, but it doesn't repeat the whole thing. I had a third part all sketched out, but when I got to it I thought, "Well, this is a lot of nonsense. The first way is the best."

Would you use a word like "rondo" to describe the last movement of the quintet?

I wouldn't use any word. I'd just tell what happens. Of course, Strauss called *Til Eulenspiegel* a rondo. I would say it was a set of variations, if you like. In the quintet there are references, which are quite literal references sometimes. But these things are like three stanzas. They're identifiable, but they're not at all literal repetitions. (I really like this piece very much as I look at it.) I would say that essentially my conception—now take this in a somewhat remote sense—I think of a big work as drama.

I noticed again the primary and secondary symbols you used in your symphonies and in your second quartet. You said you put them in afterwards as a guide for the performers.

I've given them up now, because there's no substitute for really understanding the music. Really no substitute. And those things are *very* rough indications of what you want. For instance, in the *fugato* in the second quartet, I put the principal line *not* with the theme. It depends on the piece. Now, I wouldn't apply this to the last movement of the *Hammerklavier* Sonata. I think there the theme really almost always has to be brought out, but I would say in performing a Bach fugue, the fugue subject is the last thing that needs to be brought out, because it's there and you don't miss it.

It's the music, of course, it's always the music that has to be brought out, but sometimes the way to do that is to emphasize the theme. We've been studying the C-sharp minor quartet in my graduate course, and that's one thing I point out: The theme *doesn't* need to be always hammered out. I learned that many, many years ago. Once when I was playing the *Kunst der Fuge* for two pianos with a friend, there was a point where I had to come in with the theme and there was a beautiful line going on in the other piano. The other pianist suddenly got very soft when that line should have been soaring up. These markings are such a rough, makeshift way of indicating things, that I've pretty much given it up.

The quintet is a wonderful medium. You add a viola, and you get twenty times the resources. Of course, I think the quintets of Mozart are at the very, very top. Perhaps, from my standpoint the quintet is better writing for the medium, although the second quartet is perfectly all right, too. But I think the quartet may be a more important piece—I'm not sure.

As I remember it, the music in the first violin of the quintet is the first hexachord.

In order?

Yes. And this second hexachord in viola two is treated rather freely, as I remember it. As a matter of fact, these first four notes were the first idea I had. I thought of that beginning for several years before I wrote the quintet. I remember I was walking in Berkeley one day. I decided this was going to be the way my next chamber piece began—these first four notes.

We're studying in my course Beethoven's A-minor quartet, op. 132, this year. That is very much the same kind of movement, although I've never related it to the quintet. I've related it to the first movement of my first quartet sometimes, because the three sections are really sort of variations. Both the ideas occur. I think I really like my second quartet better, but I like the quintet, too, very much. I think the quintet is a marvelous medium. I've found that, as far as color goes, one viola makes more difference than simply a quarter of the whole business.

Were the Six Pieces for Cello commissioned?

No, this was something I set myself. I thought of the instrument and what it could do, and little by little ideas that I really liked began to take shape. And the names came later, of course, after I had finished them. But I think the names are rather accurate.

I understood five of the six names—Prelude, Scherzo, Berceuse, Fantasy, and Epilogue. But I couldn't decide exactly which two elements the second one, Dialogue, was between.

The phrases contrast. Up to tempo I is the first phrase. Like a conversation, not questions and answers. This is the most difficult one to perform. Not to play, but to interpret. I've been told that it sounded like a conversation. And I can't tell you which is me and which is someone else. But it has to be done rather delicately with these contrasts. There's a lot of this business in it, you see. You could arrange the different elements of the Dialogue in different ways. I mean, it's not an argument. The *più mosso* is a variation of the opening, as is the tempo I.

The title came later. But I think that if you think of it as a dialogue, that helps the performer. Let's say I start to talk about a certain subject, and then someone comments about it at some length, and then I say, "But." (My daughter used to say, when she was a little girl, "I hate that word, 'but.'")

Qualifiers, get them out!

Well, it could have several senses. It's certainly a very friendly dialogue.

And were these written in this particular order, or did you switch the order around?

No, I don't think they were, or I've forgotten which order. Maybe the first one was written first, because I remember having that first idea very early in the game. One day I'd work on one, another day I'd work on another. Of course, one doesn't remember that clearly just exactly what happened.

The Berceuse has very definite associations. That's after my granddaughter was born and I saw her in the crib. I saw her lying in the crib and immediately I thought of that opening. I'd say they're very intimate pieces. They're very difficult.

I was looking more specifically at the use of the row.

They're quite strict with the row.

In the violin sonata and the third piano sonata and here at the very end of this piece, you seem to like to use the retrograde to finish off the piece.

Also in the cantata. What many people would not like to admit is that the row is a musical entity, too. A very important musical entity. I sort of discover the row as I go on, in a way, discover its possibilities and what it contains. It's on that basis that all the variations develop.

I was thinking in terms of specific intervals. Several of the movements begin or end with the perfect fourth, perfect fifth, which is the beginning of the row, after all. No. 4 starts with the retrograde of the row, utilizing the third quite a bit.

After all, the musical ideas, or if you like, motives, develop quite independently. I won't say independently of the row exactly, but they generate other ideas.

> It was particularly striking to me after having examined the first three movements and arriving at the fourth movement to see all these thirds that hadn't been exploited in the preceding movements. The interval of a fourth is very definitely a unifying feature of many of the movements.

Of course, a row is really as much a set of relationships, at least as much, perhaps much more, as it is a series of notes. Intervals. And then very often the final interval of one transposition will be the beginning interval of the next. You've got to connect these things. You don't always want just six notes, or just twelve notes, you want more than that. That plays very much of a role. And you have to get the ones you want, because you hear them first and then you find them. You may find them in several places; one place is more appropriate than another.

In Schoenberg's use of the row, which was more varied and richer than any of the others in a way—I mean I'm not sure, I haven't checked up on this in the music of Dallapiccola, for instance, or of my own—if you interpret the row vertically, then that leads to other forms. Because what are you going to do with a broken chord? Well, that opens up a lot of possibilities so that you might almost say the sky is the limit. It is, really. If a—I don't like the word "system," but if a set, which is I suppose, a better term—if a set of notes doesn't contain all possible things, you come to limits. Then in a musical vocabulary you've got to extend the limits as far as possible. As far as they will make sense, obviously; I mean you don't do this arbitrarily. There's always got to be musical sense there. The row doesn't change the fundamental nature of music at all. That's why I've sometimes referred to it as a convenience. If the row is convenient for a composer, then it's justified. If it's inconvenient, it's not. That's putting it in the most low-key way possible. But it's the possibilities you find in it, not the limitations. If you have the right attitude, and that involves discipline, too—then the limitations fulfill its purpose. I've said somewhere, and I believe this thoroughly, that the fact that some first-class composers have found the row convenient is ample justification—in fact it's the only possible justification for it.

There are some individuals who write for the press; those are the only ones I know, but I'm sure there are others, too, to whom when you mention the row that immediately condemns everything. Some of my not-friends on the *New York Times* do that always. They say serialism is passé now; it isn't passé, obviously. But a certain attitude toward it is quite passé. Provided that attitude is rigid, I say let's say goodbye to it without regrets, although it might come back in individual situations. A piece that's based on a very strict use of the row isn't at all by that formula a bad piece. Maybe somebody will do it again sometime and produce very good results. But if it becomes a dogma, of course, a dogma is always bad. It doesn't live very long. You kiss it goodbye without regrets.

Your Canons are dedicated to the memory of Stravinsky.

It isn't the same kind of canon all the way through. Sometimes it's a canon by inversion. It's awfully easy to write a canon, but the problem is to make some real music out of it, not have it just a canon.

It's a muted string quartet. Is the notion of muting the quartet part of the elegy, if you will, for Stravinsky, or . . . ?

Why I muted it? No, it's simply that that seemed the character of the music. And I wanted to make it as simple as possible, and it's a reasonably modest little piece.

I sketched a lot of other canons before I made this one and they're perfectly good canons, but they seemed a little irrelevant for the purpose.

Could you identify the ways in which they seemed irrelevant, and this one didn't? What was it about them?

I was writing a canon, instead of writing music, so to speak, or it came to the point where I was. That's all. I didn't want to write something in memory of Stravinsky that was simply perfunctory. Different people take these things in different ways. With the row, the easiest thing in the world to write is a canon. I would never do a thing like that simply for its own sake. I have to have a musical idea to start with, one that appeals to me.

I was looking at the new Five Pieces for Piano. They do look difficult to play.

Eddy Cone said he's been practicing them, and he said they're very hard. They're much harder than my third sonata. But they're shorter, of course.

About how long would this be in performance? I didn't figure it out from the metronome markings.

I suppose about twelve minutes. It's impossible really to figure metronome marks out, because they give a sort of mean indication of tempo. I mean, tempo is such a relative thing. It depends on the player. It depends on the hall. I would mind if measures 14 and 15 were not accurate here. But I think it shouldn't be any faster than quarter note equals 72.

The tempi and rhythms are so specifically notated here within a certain relative framework, would you mind if there were variations? In other words, if it were slower than that?

No. I don't think I would take it much slower, but that also depends on the pianist. I mean, some performers can sustain a very slow tempo, an incredibly slow tempo, and it's absolutely full of electricity all the time.

I think the rhythm is one of the features of it that are so interesting. Here it is similar in some respects to the third piano sonata, in that the polyrhythms give a sensation that the hands, or voices, are moving in different tempi from one another, a sort of rhythmic stratification of counterpoint.

Unfortunately, that's my disease. It gets worse and worse. [laughter]

It's progressed quite nicely here. It's at an acute stage.

I'm not trying to get over it.

Nothing that needs to be cured, necessarily, but it's at a pretty complicated stage. It's notated very precisely with rhythmic meanings. That would seem to create a "problem" in notating the original musical idea.

The bar lines are sometimes quite difficult. In fact, I had a page of orchestral score of the Ninth Symphony practically done last week, and then I decided that one of the bar lines was in the wrong place and so I discarded it and copied it all down again, which was quite a job.

We've talked before about bar lines and the tyranny of the downbeat. I also mean the rhythmic subdivisions and the fives against fours, and the fives against threes, and things like that. I think that you would have to have a good vocabulary of what's pianistic and what a performer could read most easily.

So many things to think of. And in fact that's been a problem since the First Symphony. Almost since I wrote *The Black Maskers*.

In the first movement of my duo there's a place where the piano is playing triplets steadily. The violin is playing a melody against it. In some places I carried a triplet *over* the bar line—I mean, I had the first two notes in one measure and the third note in the other measure. And the result was that when I played it, even with Rudolf Kolisch, we had to spend more time on those two pages than on the whole rest of the piece. It's not a too good idea in an ensemble work. In a piano work it wouldn't be, either, but I've never done it since then.

In the Five Pieces your notations are wonderfully explicit.

Of course, fifty years of experience is a great help.

People always ask, "What can a composition teacher teach a student, really?" It seems things like this are what you could teach a student. You can see the student's musical idea and say, "But, no, it should be notated this way, it's clearer." That's something that's part of a technique that could be communicated in a lesson. Whereas most people are in a fog about what goes on in composition lessons.

Well, if anybody asks me how you can teach composition, I say I haven't got the slightest idea. Which is wholly candid, I assure you. You have gifted students around you and you help them as much as you can, that's all. And of course, you have ungifted students, and that's much harder work, because you don't really teach them anything. But I can help naturally on things like that sometimes. Generally, what I do is make them tell me as clearly as possible what they want and then I help them to get it. The thing is, this is very elusive.

When you started the first movement of the Five Pieces up in Franconia, did you envision five movements, or did you just start and see where it took you?

I knew that there would be other pieces. And I knew that they'd be contrasting. I must have had some ideas about them, but I wanted another very slow one, which is the last one, of course. And to mention a secret forbidden subject, they're all in the same row.

Needless to say, I had looked around for it. There are chords in which the whole chromatic scale is used up very rapidly.

It is entirely the consequence of using all the chromatic intervals. The point is that *that* is the way in which you achieve really solid logic, because on that depends the kinds of contrasts you get. And on that depends basically the material of the piece. It's very hard to put that into words.

Several people who know Dallapiccola's piano works have noted a resemblance to yours in certain places—like the opening.

It would be very hard to say exactly what the difference or even the similarity is. Although I found him certainly as congenial a composer as I have ever met, I felt more and more that we were really not that much alike. The idea of dedicating the Five Pieces to him came at the very last moment, before they were published. I didn't even think of no. 4 in that connection before he died. No, that's not true. The connection with Dalla-piccola is purely coincidental. I never think of him as a composer for piano especially. He played the piano, but he wrote very, very little for piano. I think of him more as a composer for voices and for small groups and instruments. Of course, he was extremely good at whatever he did. I really don't know his piano writing well at all. I do know his vocal writing. I know the variations that he wrote for his daughter, which he later orchestrated.

The reference to him at the beginning of the fourth piece I put down because I was thinking of him part of the time when I was writing it. I wrote down measures 13–15 and then later thought, "Why don't I dedicate the whole thing to him, to his memory?"

You yourself are a pianist . . .

I was once. I haven't touched the piano for about twenty-five years. Well, I've touched it, but not with any serious designs on it. [laughter] I haven't made love to it, let's say.

Is it possible to think of any of the Five Pieces for Piano as orchestrated?

No. I'll tell you that's a rather interesting question, because in the first place I've only written for piano when I was thinking of the piano as an instrument with a certain very specific tone quality I've had in mind. Not always quite the same one. My first piano sonata is very different from the second one, and the third is still different. It's been an entirely unconventional approach. It's interesting, because I've had very gifted people who were also extremely good pianists. I found always that they wrote very conventionally for the piano without any real sense of tone quality. That surprised me, perhaps because I was always an amateur pianist really, although Hindemith told me once that Schnabel was very proud of what I did with the piano after he got me under his claws.

I've sometimes thought of orchestrating piano works—not mine—but I found that it was absolutely impossible for me to get what I want on any other instrument. If I thought of the music in terms of the orchestra, these pieces wouldn't make certain demands on the pianists.

They do make extensive requirements on the pianist. Is the necessary awkwardness of execution part of your plan, part of the sound of the pieces?

Pianists have to learn to do it so that it's not awkward.

There are passages in Beethoven which sound awkward, because perhaps they were meant to.

I can talk quite a bit about that. I read once an interview with Horowitz and he said that Beethoven was a great composer, but his piano music simply wasn't pianistic. I thought, "What does he mean by that stupid remark?" Anybody who could make the piano ring out, the way for instance the last movement of opus 111 does in the variations, wrote pianistically. Writing well for an instrument doesn't mean that the music is always easy to play, it means that it really makes that instrument sound the way it can sound.

They never played the *Hammerklavier* when I was young. I played it by myself in my own inimitable way. Mainly the first three movements: I could do something with the first movement, with the scherzo, and with the slow movement especially. And I wanted very much to hear it. There wasn't even a recording, but there was a recording of an orchestral version made by Felix Weingartner. I played it and this recording was very disappointing, because everything was easy.

> *In a sense the struggle is embodied in the writing and is not meant to be removed. The kind of tension that goes into playing a difficult passage* itself *communicates to the audience.*

It's not as if Beethoven weren't a first-class pianist himself, after all; he was.

> *So the struggle to accommodate the difficult rhythms and other difficult passages in the Five Pieces is built in. It's part of the drama of the piece; it's not just the music on the page, but the performer playing it and the audience listening to it.*

3

Vocal
Music

On the Beach at Fontana was written for a volume of songs that were published and were given to James Joyce on his fiftieth birthday. And there's a very funny story about that. It's a poem about—I interpret it as an older woman who loved a younger man, and they're walking on the beach in Italy and there's a storm coming up. She feels very protective. So I set it for soprano and piano.

Well, the man who played my first sonata came to Rome, where I was working on the sonata, and I showed him this piece. And he said, "But you set it for soprano—that's a homosexual song." And I said, "Well, I felt there was something not quite right, but that's the only way I could interpret it." So I left it for soprano.

So the song was published and sung. Then, several years later, when I was back in New York in the mid-thirties, I was invited by a lady to come and have tea—one had tea in those days—and she said a singer named Radiana Pasmor would be there. The lady said, "Please bring your song, because in the first place, the son and daughter-in-law of Joyce will be there, and Mrs. Pasmor would like to sing it." And I said, "Well, I don't think it can be read at sight." And she said, "Well, *she* can." (I'd never heard of a singer who could read at sight at that time. They're much better trained musically now.) I took it over and she *did* sing it at sight. She looked it over at first and then we just played it.

And then I went and sat next to Mrs. Joyce, who said, "I'm awfully happy to meet you, and I'm awfully happy that you set that song, because this is my favorite poem of my father-in-law's. You know, it was written for my husband." Well, of course, never having had children myself, I couldn't imagine that it was about a father and his son!

Have you read Robert Cogan's analysis of this song? [1] *In it the author ranks pitches according to the relative height of the vowel sounds. Were you consciously thinking of the* i *in "wind" and the* i *in "shingle" as being high on this scale?*

I don't think of it. I mean, I think I have a feeling for words, in fact I know I have, because I'm very much aware of words and of the sound of them, and the rhythm of course, but what a musical analysis does and what a composer does—they're the opposite things, of course.

You have composed two operas. What prompted you to write your first opera, The Trial of Lucullus?

Henry Schnitzler, the son of the Austrian writer Arthur Schnitzler, was in the drama department at Berkeley, where I taught. He's one of my best friends still. He was the one who got this whole thing started. One of his jobs was to give a production every spring. He came to me up at Lake Tahoe, where we were for the summer, and he said he wanted to put on two musical works in the spring: one was *l'Histoire du Soldat* of Stravinsky, and the other was an opera by Sessions. I said, "Well, that's very well, but there is no opera by Sessions." He said, "Will you write one?" And I said, "I have no text." He said, "I'll find you a text." And he thought of Brecht, who is very sympathetic to me. I think it's a wonderful text myself. Brecht sent him this radio play.

Brecht also gave a German version to another composer—I've known him for years—Paul Dessau, unbeknownst to me and mine unbeknownst to him. The week after this was first performed—it was performed three times on each of two successive weeks—one of my students came to me and asked if I knew Paul Dessau. I said, "Oh, yes." And he said, "I saw him in Los Angeles and he wouldn't believe me when I said you were in Berkeley, because he said, 'He lives in Princeton.' I told him you're here; I heard your opera *The Trial of Lucullus* last weekend. And Dessau said, 'That *proves* he's not in Berkeley, because *I'm* writing that.'"

Of course, Dessau and Brecht moved to East Germany, and they wouldn't let them perform it with this text, they made them change the text. I think they ruined the text, myself. A lot of other people do, too. This is a wonderful text. I asked a friend of mind in Germany why Brecht's text was banned, because it was against war and so forth. He said, "Well, it's against war, but the Russians are against war when the Americans make it, but they're for it when they make it."

There are a lot of corrections in your score.

To be sure, my vocal score was done at lightning speed, and the manuscript looks absolutely by far the most dreadful looking manuscript I ever produced. The published version is full of mistakes.

This was performed not in a theater but in a large lecture hall at Berkeley, and there was room for only a certain number of players. I had five woodwinds: that is, a flute and an oboe, which in one scene plays the English horn, clarinet, bass clarinet, and bassoon, which in the first five scenes plays the contrabassoon.

There was a pupil of mine who was a very good bassoon player; he was going to play the bassoon in the orchestra. I said, "Will you play the contrabassoon?" And he said, "Well I've never seen a contrabassoon, but there's one around here." So one day we went over to the women's gym at Berkeley, where the contrabassoon was kept in a huge trunk, got out the contrabassoon, and he cuddled up to it and found he could play it all right. And then he came to me one day and said, "We've got a problem, because the contrabassoon comes in the fifth scene—how are we going to warm it up before-hand?" And I said, "I guess I'll have to introduce it in the first scene."

We had *all* sorts of adventures. Because this was entirely volunteer work, and people would drop out sometimes. One night when I was at dinner the whole cello section collapsed, and I was rather desperate. I called up a lady who was a cellist; she knew all the cellists in the region, and I told her my problem. She asked if I'd asked my oculist. His name was Owen Dixon. I said I wouldn't *dream* of asking him to do this, because it's a lot of work, and he's a very busy man. She called back and said to call him. So I gave him a ring and told him what the whole problem was. He asked, "When's the next rehearsal?" And I said, "In forty-five minutes." He said, "Would you mind if I were a little late?" All sorts of things happened, but we got through it all right.

Were the instruments related to individual characters in the opera?

In certain places. The Fishwife's song, for instance, is the most emotional moment in the opera, I suppose. There's an oboe which accompanies her; it doesn't so much accompany, it plays all the interludes. In the sixth scene one character has the English horn. During the performance the English horn entered and let out a little peep and then collapsed entirely and broke his reed. I thought, "My God, what's going to happen now?" You see, it's a small orchestra, and everything is very much exposed. Well, when I got to the next passage for the English horn, I was amazed to hear it come on the clarinet. And I had to go on conducting; I mean, you can't do anything, you just have to use your wits. I thought, "Over here somewhere I need both the clarinet and the English horn. What's going to happen then?" I saw the clarinet player whispering in the ear of the oboe player, and when the time came, he took up his oboe and played the English horn part on the oboe. I've told that story on both sides of the Atlantic; it makes a big impression on everybody, because they'd never heard of anything quite like that. So when the clarinet player was up for a very posh fellowship when he was a graduate student at Harvard, he gave me as a reference, and I wrote them and told them all about it. I said it showed that he was a very resourceful man. He got the posh fellowship and is now a rather distinguished professor of philosophy at Harvard—Stanley Cavell.

> *One thing that I noticed throughout* The Trial of Lucullus *was what I would call word-painting, or in the baroque sense, affections: the idea of portraying in the music what the character is speaking about.*

Of course, naturally. I do that always.

> *How much of that carried over into your instrumental music? Were there things that you were thinking, almost in a programmatic sense . . . ?*

No. Oh, faintly sometimes. There is a passage in my Second Symphony that I always call "the atomic bomb." It was a sort of catastrophic moment in the last movement. My Second Symphony is very much connected in my mind with the Second World War, and of course it's dedicated to the memory of Roosevelt. If these things are on one's mind, they come in. But they come in one's feelings—I think the musical ideas come first and then one associates them.

> *That was said about the* Pastoral *Symphony, that Beethoven wrote the music first and then named the movements.*

I wonder. He probably did both more or less together, but the music is the more important thing. And in a dramatic work, in the cantata [*When Lilacs Last in the Dooryard Bloom'd*], the words carry a power in themselves as they go along, you see.

After all, that goes through music history. It doesn't belong in the nineteenth century only. Music is not an isolated thing in one's consciousness, it's one's whole life, if one is really involved in it. If one sits down to write a pretty little piece of music, that's one thing. But if you're seriously involved with your music, everything goes into it. I mean, Beethoven wouldn't have dedicated his Fourth Symphony to Napoleon, or even thought of it.

Everything in one's life, more or less, is involved in it. Sometimes one is aware of this, and sometimes one isn't. Most of the time, I suppose, in a way one isn't. People have pointed out about the *Meistersinger,* which is the one really quite cheerful piece Wagner ever wrote, that at the time he was having the worst time in his own life.

But you'd probably be glad to write a cheerful piece at that time.

Of course, one is involved in the subject. It wasn't because I was feeling sad that I wrote the cantata. I wasn't thinking of anybody's assassination except Lincoln's when I started that second part, but then Martin Luther King was shot; and then Bobby Kennedy was shot—and his funeral train was passing through while I was writing the second part, and I was affected by it.

You once noted that the Fourth Symphony incorporates a thrush's song,[2] as does the cantata.

I think it was a wood thrush. That was not by malice aforethought at all; it just found its way into it. It's the general idea of a hermit thrush's song, you know, because every thrush has different notes. The actual song of the hermit thrush is more varied than it is in this music. There didn't seem to be any sense in trying to change this radically every time.

Did you hear this bird up in Franconia?

More there than anywhere else. I heard it first in Williamsburg, Massachusetts. The bird doesn't come down that far south, generally. The reason they call it the hermit thrush is because you find it mostly in deep woods. Where we lived in Franconia, the woods were not really that deep, but they were all around the houses there. We didn't hear it near our house, but we had neighbors who lived a little higher up the hill than we did, and one could hear it there. If we had gone further out, we could have heard it still more. It's not an uncommon bird at all, but it comes in that kind of a landscape.

The Whitman poem about Lincoln reads, "a shy and hidden bird."

And in this book *Specimen Days* of Whitman he mentions having heard the hermit thrush in a certain place on Long Island. That's further south than it generally goes—it's not so common there. In the Connecticut valley, one didn't hear it. We didn't even have the wood thrush very much. In fact, I don't ever remember having heard the wood thrush in Northampton. We had all sorts of other birds.

You are very attentive to birds.

I have been at various times. But I was more interested as a child than I am now. I enjoyed listening in Europe to the nightingale, although the main thing about the nightingale is that it sings incessantly and it sings at night. There's a lot of variety, but it doesn't have the very, very special tone quality that the American thrushes have. The Wilson's thrush has a quite different kind of call. The wood thrush has a call of three notes [whistles], but it has a very special characteristic color. The Wilson's thrush goes [whistles]. And the hermit thrush is like a coloratura wood thrush with much more life and exuberance. It starts on a long note [whistles] as it does in the cantata.

After the cantata was performed in Boston, some of the people in the chorus who come from the western part of Massachusetts said it sounded just like the thrushes in their backyards. But I wasn't trying to reproduce the hermit thrush. I was suggesting the kind of sound that Whitman refers to. That may seem a very, very fine distinction, but there's nothing that literal about it. In other words, I didn't look it up, or anything like that.

Turn, O Libertad was written for a special occasion. This was during the war, of course. The man who was in charge of music at the Temple Emanu-El arranged programs, each a salute to one of the Allies. I got Russia. And I chose this Whitman poem with some malice aforethought, addressed to Russia. I wrote it very fast. Because this was written for an occasion and for a special group, I didn't want it to be too difficult. It was more difficult than I'd intended it to be, but I can't help that. It might be a good idea if some people read that poem nowadays.

The Whitman text says, "Liberty wins out in the end always." It lasts about three or four minutes; it's a very short poem. It's not one of Whitman's very good poems; it just has an irreproachable sentiment to it. There's the word "caste," and it rhymes with "past." The idea was: "We throw off the feudal past and abolish caste." It was very nice. A little chorus in Darmstadt did it.

> You mentioned once carrying the text around in your mind memorized, and finding occasionally that the original words might be transposed in your mental version. That happened in the cantata.

Yes, I had "and" instead of "with." "And a thousand voices rising strong and solemn." And I had "the gloomy pines so still." I had to change it to "the ghostly pines so still." I carry the text around in my mind and I carry its meaning. I wrote "the swamp odors." "The swamp perfume" is correct. It's not terribly important, but it's so easy to make those mistakes and that may have happened with the text of *Lucullus*. I did that with the *Idyll of Theocritus* in a couple of places, too. In some cases I transposed words, and I kept the transposition, because of the rhythm. I thought of the line in those terms. Maybe I did that in the cantata even, and I don't think Walt Whitman will mind.

> *How much rewriting of the* Idyll of Theocritus *did you do?*

I didn't rewrite anything, as I remember. I did what I've always done with vocal music: I've sketched the vocal part primarily and sketched the rest of it in a very sketchy way and then worked it out later, and not always retaining it. And furthermore, when you sketch in big lines like that, as you sort of elaborate the whole thing, the lines themselves can be changed sometimes. As I sketch, I know pretty much what the orchestra is going to do. However, I could show you one instance. At the end of *Theocritus* [measure 549 in the flute] is a very special part, a sort of aria in itself, if you like. Now, I was convinced that this phrase was going to be on the oboe. When I got there, I said, "No, no, the oboe is quite wrong for that. Too much intensity in the oboe. It's the flute that I need." Things like that. I didn't make that decision till I actually got there.

That's always been the way I've written a vocal piece. Because the vocal part is predominant. I did that in *Montezuma,* too. Not in quite so thoroughgoing a manner as I did it here. I mean, I sketched that scene by scene and got the general plan in that way. Of course, with a dramatic work you have to think of the timing, the characters, and so forth.

> *I noticed several uses of instruments for various moods. Particularly the harp, for instance, with the business about the magic wheel.*

That's almost an operatic gesture, because the magic wheel is a real little thing, it is not just a figure of speech. It was a wheel of fortune. I thought of it a little in those terms.

> *There are many sections in which the music seems to mirror the text. For instance, the part where she's talking about smearing, the line smears.*

[laughter] The singer should not smear the line.

> *Yes, but her voice undulates on one syllable. There are several cases: "Pining" away, for example.*

In a way, it's a monodrama. It would be hard to stage, because there's only one character. A lot of it is in description, memories, and so forth. In a way, it belongs in the general realm of opera—it's a monodrama. I think if Schoenberg hadn't written *Erwartung,* I wouldn't have had the courage to write this, I don't know. Not that there's the slightest resemblance there in either the story or the music. But the idea of a big piece for a single voice; and of course the single voice has much more of a workout here.

> *I was looking at the two refrains, the first "O magic wheel, draw hither to my house the man I love," and the second, "Bethink thee of my love and whence it came, O holy Moon." I simply copied out the vocal line for each of those phrases and compared them. Naturally, they are never exactly the same—they're reminiscent of each other, but not the same notes, or even rhythm. And of course I was looking for some of the twelve-tone aspects of it.*

The twelve-tone aspect is very much in the background. It establishes a vocabulary, a strict mode of procedure. This is very much rhapsodical. I didn't try to follow the row absolutely through at all. It's really a motive, rather than a row. I think, as I remember, there are certain places where it becomes a row, but it isn't real twelve-tone writing in any sense of the word. I was going about that very carefully and gingerly, and this has to be rhapsodic. It has to be performed with lots of juice, after all. And with a sense of timing and so forth. And I couldn't possibly have used the twelve-tone series strictly in a rhapsodic way then. Because that implies a minute attention. There's a lot of serial thinking in this piece, but it's only one element. The whole structure isn't referable to the twelve-tone row.

> *I looked for the row in the opening vocal line, "Bethink thee of my love"; however, the second time it comes in it has all twelve tones, and the fourth time as well.*

Certainly by that time I was very sensitive to the effect of repeated tones, unless they're repeated very definitely. I tended to not repeat tones too soon, so to speak. And for years before that, before my violin sonata, this is one of the things that made me realize that I was going in that direction. I found myself being very sensitive in my students' work to notes that were repeated too quickly. This is one of the things that led to serial conception, certainly. When I say "harmonic," I'm referring not only to chords but to the relationship of all the intervals. A repeated tone tends to produce a temporary, even momentary, suspension of movement. Sometimes that's good and sometimes that's bad, but one ought to always be aware of it. It used to be said of the twelve-tone system that you weren't able to repeat tones, but of course you can.

> *Since there were, conveniently, twelve textual refrains of "Bethink thee of my love," I initially thought they might be transpositions of the same thing. Some of them begin on $B^{\natural}$ some on $B^{\flat}$ . . .*

Well, it's just this ascending line.

> *Right. It maintains the contour, but I was getting frustrated because I was trying to make it fit a more serialized notion than it is. And of course the intervals would get off by half a step or something . . .*

Probably one has to look for the notes in order to prove that it's not very important. It's the line and it's the context in which it appears that's important. Simaitha has different ways of saying, "Bethink thee of my love." Sometimes it's a nostalgic sense, and sometimes it's distressed; sometimes it's agitated, sometimes it's sort of by the side. Once it is almost triumphant, because she's thinking of when things actually came to pass. Of course, she's interrupting what she says, the flowery speech.

A very intelligent former student of mine drove me back from a talk I gave at the University of Chicago. She said she's always been puzzled by Delphis's speech. She said, "You know, it just occurred to me today that Delphis isn't being serious and sincere when he makes that speech at all." And I said, "No, of course not."

Do you feel he's handing her a line?

He's flamboyant.

Is it possible that he actually meant it?

Well, he thought he meant it. He was excited, and he was offered this girl on a silver platter, and there she was. But he overdoes it, I think. What are the words? "With torches and with hammers I would have beaten down the door." [laughter]

If you think of a human situation—unfortunately, it's possible to think you're in love with somebody and really not be at all. That happens in life. I don't think much of Delphis.

There's an ambiguity that's raised at the beginning and at the end about whether the new lover is a man or a woman.

The *new* lover, I think, is the charming Philinos, whom he beat in the race. Of course, this was an open possibility in Greek civilization. It's been somewhat overinterpreted, I think, because if you take Greek literature and think of the female figure—they were wonderful. Obviously, the Greeks appreciated women very much, if you think about people like Antigone, and even Medea and Cassandra. I think of Greek tragedy, but they held the other possibilities open, too. Only, it was supposed to be on a more platonic plane, I think. I think these things are somewhat overinterpreted nowadays in certain quarters.

I was going to raise the question that, if indeed his new lover were a man, perhaps that was his initial predisposition.

That was in a pre-Freudian epoch. I mean, things were much more natural and simple.

Of course, Freud took the Greeks and unsimplified them, or desimplified them.

They weren't that simple. But they were very direct. Put it that way.

You mentioned a two-piano version of this.

Yes. The two-piano version is better than the one-piano version. The orchestral version is the real version.

You would suggest using the two-piano version over the one-piano version?

Oh yes, by far. The one-piano version I slung together because I had to have something to send out to Louisville. And it's unplayable on the piano. It's like all my piano arrangements of *Montezuma,* too. Composers aren't good arrangers of their own music. Because you don't want to leave anything out. Everything in there is essential.

This is the first work where I really went to town with the voice. You don't write for the voice as if it were the second violin. It doesn't work, except in relation to the voices. In the cantata, and in *Montezuma,* and in my biblical choruses, there are places where some of the voices are less important than others. But it is always the voices. I think this is nature, practically. You wouldn't write a concerto with vocal accompaniment. It doesn't work, that's all.

Do you feel that writing for voice in a twelve-tone system is any different from writing for voices in The Trial of Lucullus, *say?*

Not when you've learned how to do it.

Your setting is very amenable to the inflections and the speed at which certain syllables are pronounced, and to the rhythms of our language.

Of course I think all vocal music should be that way. Verdi is always like that. But it's not in four-measure phrases with tonal cadences at the end of every four measures.

What made you choose this text?

It's a long story. Mainly, I'd been interested in this poem for years and years. I heard a piece that I liked very much by a composer named Charles Martin Loeffler, a European composer who emigrated to the U. S. and was a violinist who lived in Boston. He wrote a piece called *A Pagan Poem* based on a poem by Virgil—it wasn't a vocal work at all. And it was a rather nice arrangement, because there was this woman who was calling her lover, and the lover finally appears from town, and he had a chorus of trumpets from behind the stage who represented the lover; and finally they came closer and closer and then they appeared, and I liked that at the time. I don't know how I'd like it now. I might not like it at all.

Anyway, this was nearly sixty years ago. This poem of Virgil's was an imitation of a much greater poem by Theocritus. I tried to get hold of a translation of the poem by Theocritus, and finally found one years later. It didn't interest me at all. It was a Victorian translation. As far as the two young people got was sitting on the couch and holding hands. That was the climax of the work. And I thought, "That's really not what I had been led to expect." Then I bought the poem in Greek. I can read Greek somewhat.

Then, years later, after I came back from Florence in 1952, I was waiting for a plane down on 42nd Street opposite the Grand Central Station. I knew I was going to spend the night on the plane. (It took a night to go from New York to California in 1952 still.) And I went to look for something to read. I got an anthology of Greek poems. And in that anthology was this translation by a man I had known really rather well—an Englishman. He was a friend, and I saw him very often at the Berensons' house. Trevelyan made some wonderful translations from Greek. He translated Aeschylus in the original meters. He came and read some of them out loud; they were very impressive.

So on the plane I devoured this poem. I thought, "Well, I must set some of this to music." And then I decided I've really got to set the whole thing. And of course it was a somewhat bold thing to do, to set a poem of that length. People refer to my aria, and I say, "It's not an aria, it's more like a concerto." Forty-two minutes long. Also, it's as much of a job as the role of Elektra, for instance, or at least one good act of *Tristan*. I put a lot into it, and of course I was thrilled to be writing for the voice.

I was offered a commission from Louisville, and I said, "Will you accept this?" They said they would. That's how I came to write it, really.

I wondered why you thought it was regrettable that I didn't retain the original title, *The Sorceress*.

That's because I like the title The Sorceress *better— that's my own preference.*

The Sorceress sounds a little too scholastic for me.

It sounds magical to me.

Well, I know, but it's really a love poem. The magic is part of the scenery, so to speak.

The moon goddess had three incarnations: one was Selene, one was Hecate, one was Artemis. Artemis being the most familiar one; it would be Diana in the Roman mythology. As a Greek goddess, she was somewhat different. These were three different incarnations of the moon goddess. Hecate was really a very sinister goddess—the goddess of doom, the goddess of vengeance, a very sinister character. Artemis was the majestic one.

> *You once said that, if Schoenberg hadn't written* Erwartung, *you might not have had the courage to write* Theocritus.

In a way that was a manner of speaking. I wasn't aware that it took that amount of courage. But actually, writing a forty-five minute piece for a solo soprano . . . I mean, *Elektra* is one of the most difficult operatic roles there is, and she's not singing all the time, and it lasts only an hour and a half at the very most, maybe a little more. It may be twice as long as *Theocritus,* but Elektra isn't singing by any means all the time, or half the time probably. So, *Theocritus* is a big, big job for the soprano. I never felt I had to grit my teeth to write it. I had to write it, so I wrote it.

The *Mass for Unison Choir* is a work in which I was limited in the resources that I could use. I went to the school which commissioned it, the Kent School, God knows how many years ago. They wanted something that the glee club could sing, you see. And I said, "Well, I can only do so much." They wanted the whole school congregation to be able to sing it. I said, "There's not the slightest chance that the whole school student body could sing my music." Things which come very easily and naturally to me don't always come easily and naturally to other people. The glee club lost its nerve. It had to be for unison choir and organ. I wrote it in a much more diatonic and tonal style than I usually do. But I think it has some good things in it. I've conducted it myself a number of times. It's not so easy. The trouble is, my music isn't difficult for me, but it's difficult for everybody else.

I used it with the Anglican words. They told me I could use the Greek words for the *Kyrie.* The headmaster had these ideas about the historical meaning of these texts. *Kyrie eleison* did not really mean, "Oh, God have mercy upon us miserable sinners"—that comes in the *Agnus Dei.* He said this is more like "Hail to the chief." He had his ideas about Episcopal ritual. And then he wanted the *Sursum corda,* which isn't in the regular text, so I put something together for that. I tried to follow the text. And I think it's a wonderful text, of course.

The first performance was in the Cathedral of St. John the Divine in New York. It's such a big place that you could stick St. Peter's off in one of the chapels and nobody'd notice it. Not quite true, of course, but it's a huge place, and it's got very strange acoustics. Being brought up in the Episcopal church, I know the words of the Mass very well, but I had to listen for my cues—I conducted it—and if I turned my head *that* much, I'd get the beginning of the sentence, and if I turned *that* much, I'd get the end of the sentence suddenly. It was strange acoustically. And this was compounded by the fact that the organist was as close to me as that lamp, and the choir was way, way down there. The organist was there at the keyboard, but the sound came out from New Jersey somewhere. People told me that when you got to the third measure the first measure was still sounding. So, it was a very strange experience. I think it's a rather nice piece. It's not entirely uncharacteristic, but it's unimpeachably tonal.

Was it their idea for the unison chorus, or yours?

If you take a boy's prep school—it's both boys and girls now; at that time it was only boys—who go to church and sing hymns a fifth above without very good intonation, you don't go in for very much part writing. And unison chorus was perfectly good.

I asked because the unison chorus could sound somewhat like organum, as you said, a fifth up without meaning to be.

It might, but it's not supposed to sound like that. I have got a unison chorus, or partly that, in *Montezuma*, a little one. It has its possibilities, and of course, if you write for chorus, you can always have them sing in unison sometimes.

Were any of the melodies in the choral part taken from plainchant? They have some plainchant-like rings, and some of them you could even assign a mode, if you adjusted a little bit here and there.

Well, no, not really. I like plainchant. And I know just a tiny bit about it, probably not much nowadays, but as of the 1930s I did know something about it. I had an Italian friend who was a very good vocal teacher. He insisted that the notes weren't all equal in length. According to him, it followed the Latin prosody in which there's always a difference in length between the long and the short vowels, which makes sense. But I would imagine that what actually happened was that it would sound differently in different places, probably.

I was not consciously thinking of plainchant, but a little, in a sort of a distant way. But I don't blame plainchant for anything that I wrote. [laughter] Also I think there are certain fundamental things about melody. And you find them in plainchant, you find them in music of the Renaissance. Some of it I love very much. Orlando di Lasso, especially, and Palestrina, Josquin des Prez, and Victoria, and some of the madrigal writers too.

What would you call the fundamentals of melody?

Movement of the line. That's what I mean. I don't mean four-measure phrases necessarily. They don't occur very often in my music. But I mean the contour of the musical line. The expressive contour, if you like. I think that music is more movement than sound, almost. It's movement in terms of sound. I mean without movement, there's no music. And this is the shape of the movement.

I could say that the music of the Renaissance is always in the same key, but it's in different modes. I have said that sometimes. I think the essential thing about tonality as such is the sort of recognizable principle—the "key factor," so to speak—is not the establishment of a key, but the fact that you can change the key. I think modulation is the basic factor in tonality, as distinguished from what came before it, and as distinguished from what came after it. Because in a contemporary idiom quote unquote—I mean, I shudder a little every time I use a term like that—you can't modulate, you can't change a key. You can get very sharp momentary contrasts, but you can't sustain them over a long period. The whole means of contrast are different in my own musical idiom. That's all I would say. You can get a very sharp contrast here, but the nature of the harmonic clusters, or harmonies, or whatever you want to call them, is that all the harmonies tend to become, from, the tonal point of view, ambiguous. The contrast is a striking moment. You're not really changing the locality, so to speak, of the music. You can change it by having it in a high register as opposed to having it in a low register, but you can't change the harmonic focus, because it's much more complicated. You can use a transposition of the row, but *that* doesn't do that kind of a trick at all; that does something else. It brings another kind of contrast.

In the Mass there are very long phrases, of course. In that way there's some influence of Gregorian chant, I suppose. And the phrases follow very much the phrases of the texts. Of course, that's inevitable in the nature of the text itself, because it's a series of statements, especially the *Credo* and the *Gloria*. And the sections, so-called, follow the paragraphs of the text.

For instance, on the word "buried" this G is, I think, the lowest pitch that you use. Very deep for that word.

Of course, this is so completely natural. If you ascend into Heaven, the music goes up. If you descend into Hell, the music goes down. It would be ridiculous to have it the other way. I'm sure there are people who would do it the other way, because they would think they were doing something new that way. [laughter]

Since the Latin of this text has been set so often, did you feel at all inhibited by having to work with the English rather than the Latin?

Well, I tried to forget the Latin. Of course, I know the Latin text very, very well, too. I know Beethoven's *Missa Solemnis* by heart, Bach's B-minor Mass not quite by heart, but very well. Of course, Palestrina and the *Penitential Psalms* of Orlando di Lasso. In answer to your question, no, I didn't. Of course, having been brought up as the grandson of a bishop in a very Episcopalian family, I know this text rather well, too. In fact, I knew it before I knew the Latin. Of course, the Latin text of the Mass—God help anybody who tried to translate it into any other language and use the same music for it. Especially the *Agnus Dei* and the *Credo.*

In works with text do you concern yourself with musical programmatic portrayals of that text?

Well, not programmatic; but if you have a very excited scene in an opera, you don't write quiet music to it, unless there's some reason for tremendous irony in the situation. I mean, you're thinking of the drama. I suppose in a way, since opera was what first fired my imagination musically, I supposed I tend toward it. My music tends to be very dramatic always. But of course, a big musical work does have a dramatic side to it. Otherwise operas would never have been written. Well, that goes way back to the Greeks, of course, at least. The Chinese, too, probably two thousand years before the Greeks.

Recitatives and arias started to go out with Mozart even, although he had *recitativo secco* and even spoken words if the text was in German. And it certainly went out with Beethoven—well, he had spoken words, too—but with Weber. *Euryanthe* especially, which is a marvelous work, unfortunately very difficult to stage convincingly. It's an absolutely wonderful work that I've always loved all my life, although I've only heard a live performance once, and that was not with the staging. It was two or three years ago in Carnegie Hall.

My vocal style is arioso, I suppose really, but it's always melodic. That's the character of my own melodic line. My meeting and friendship with Dallapiccola gave me a very great impulse to go in much more for vocal music. Naturally, in my own way and in my own language.

In The Trial, *in each case the jurors' music leads up to the music of the witnesses. Do you consider it a sort of prologue?*

Yes. The text demands that. It does that in some moments in *Montezuma,* too. I mean, there are short quasi-set numbers in that, even. And if anybody wants to call it an aria, he can. I would prefer it *myself,* even to say that Montezuma sings an aria in the second act, certainly. Because he talks for a long time, and it's a very definite expressive vocal line. Cortez and Malinche each have an aria in the last scene of the first act. She's comparing her religious beliefs to the Christian religious beliefs, and she asks him who he really is, whether he's the white God returned. He says he doesn't think he comes from hell, but he doesn't come from heaven either. But it's a dramatic aria in each case. It has been sung out of context, as the very last scene of *Montezuma* alone has been sung out of context, although generally with the whole scene, because the chorus interrupts.

And then there's the chorus of clouds at the end of the opera which concludes it, which sort of sums up the whole situation. But I don't think these are set numbers. They're integrated into the flow of the whole thing. The nearest to set numbers would be those two songs of Malinche and Cortez in the last scene of the first act. But even those are integrated.

I was interested that you said that Sprechstimme *was invented in a Viennese theater.*

It was a certain method of delivery that was in the *Volkstheater* there.

In your vocal music you've never used this technique for very long passages.

No. I like real singing. And that applies to *Montezuma,* too. In Alban Berg, it's written for real singers, too.

But aren't there parts in Wozzeck *where the pitches are indicated by an X? For instance, Marie's lullaby scene.*

I think there are. I haven't looked at the score for years. There's one scene especially where that's done. I think that *Sprechstimme* is really for the German language, not for other languages at all. In that theater, apparently it's very traditional. It goes back a long time. That was where it originated after all.

> *I'd never thought of it that way, but perhaps it's because the German language is so phonetic—every consonant sounds, every vowel. Only the "h" is silent in German. It's not like French, where so many words could sound like other words with just the slightest difference in pronunciation.*

Well, French has long vowels; naturally, sometimes German does, too.

Especially in a dramatic work like *Montezuma,* there are all sorts of things to talk about in music that have to do with the fact that it is dramatic work. And as I go through it, the music is extremely connected with the drama. Unfortunately, in the Berlin performance that wasn't very clear, because things didn't happen when I wanted them to and the whole staging was different from what I had in mind.

Hollreiser conducted, who's conducting at the Metropolitan. He's a good conductor, but he's dull, very dull. I felt he didn't really have a conception of how my music should sound—a conductor should do that. He knew nothing else that I'd written, and it was a dull performance.

> *You told me that you started thinking about* Montezuma *years before you even started writing it.*

Yes. Of course, I was working on it sporadically all that time, but what I was doing was reading over the text, making sketches mostly of the vocal parts, because, after all, an opera is a vocal work. And then thinking about the characters and then the necessary cutting of the text. I don't know exactly how much of it I cut out; it might have been as much as half of it.

The librettist, Borgese, was almost my best friend the whole time. Especially at the beginning. He was married at our house. I was his best man. This was his second wife; his first wife had died, and he married the daughter of Thomas Mann, who was living in Princeton. We gave them their wedding dinner. They were married on Thanksgiving Day, which was our wedding anniversary, too, our third, I guess. So they and the Manns and the "bridesmaid," who was a German novelist named Hermann Broch, all came to lunch at our house, and then we all went to dinner at the Manns' that evening. I saw Borgese for the last time in the spring of 1952 in Milano.

When did he first present you with the idea for the libretto?

I'm quite sure it was in 1935. I saw him just after he'd returned from a trip to Mexico. And he was bowled over by Mexico itself and by the history of Mexico, and he proposed this to me at that time. I didn't know anything about Mexico, I regret to say. But I did have a volume, I think the first edition, of Prescott's *Conquest of Mexico*. It was a book that was given to my grandfather, perhaps by Prescott himself, I don't know.

I went to California that summer for the first time, and I took Prescott with me and I was enthralled by it. I read it through, and then later, I forget whether it was that year or the following year, I read the account by Bernál Díaz which is the basis of the text of *Montezuma*. I told him when I came back, "Of course I'll do this." And I even began making sketches.

The first measure of *Montezuma* is based on the first sketch I made.

I was thinking of the figure of the old man. Then little by little we discussed the text. It took Borgese six years to write it, and we discussed all sorts of things. We discussed the characters. We discussed what kind of a person Malinche must have been. I don't think that either of us realized that her memory's a disgrace in Mexico because she helped the Spaniards at first. Because she thought Cortez was Quetzalcoatl. We discussed Montezuma himself. I mean, I'd always heard of Montezuma as a kind of weakling. We decided it wasn't quite like that—there was religious confusion.

In 1941 I got a complete copy of the text, which was huge. I read the text over to groups of students several times. I found it took me three or four hours to read it through. And it should have taken at most one hour.

I sketched through about 903 measures, a little more

than half-way through the first act, and then I decided, "Well, this can't go on this way. I've really got to cut it drastically." So I cut and I made sketches at the same time. A lot of scenes were essentially sketched out, whole episodes—but putting them all together and working them into the whole was a very big job, and I didn't finally get started on that till the end of 1959. In the first place, he'd given me four acts. *Otello* is four acts, but normally four acts is an awfully long opera. There are operas in five acts, but they put them together nowadays.

He had asked me before the text was finished, before it was delivered, how long the text should be. Well, that was very late in the day. I counted the words, very roughly of course, in *Otello*. I found it was about 10,000 words. Then I counted the words in the first act of *Götterdämmerung,* which is, as you know, extremely long. I found it was almost as long as the text of *Otello.* Anyway, I gave him the figure of 10,000 words, but as far as I could make out there were between 30,000 and 40,000 words in the text of *Montezuma.*

So I had to cut, and I started by cutting words out, and then cutting lines out, shortening long speeches—I knew they couldn't be that long in an opera. And then I found that wasn't sufficient. I finally had to eliminate a very, very nice scene for which I had written the music, because it just couldn't work.

I was working on the second act. I saw Borgese's wife in Princeton, and she asked me how it was getting on. I said, "It's very bad. It's pretty well done. I've finished pretty well with the second and third acts, but I don't know what to do with the first two acts, because somehow I've got to make one act of them." She said, "I'll help you. I'll do it for you." I told her, "All right, it should be readable through in roughly twenty minutes, because it shouldn't last more than an hour." As it is, each act lasts between forty-five and fifty minutes. She sent me back in a couple of weeks what she'd done.

Well, there were several things that didn't satisfy me. One problem especially that I didn't know how to solve—I wasn't sure that I had a very clear idea of how it could be solved. I asked Francis Fergusson if he'd advise me, which he did. He said he thought that one of the scenes in the first act was superfluous, just to leave that scene out entirely. It seemed to me to be an awfully important scene, but as things shaped up, this was very, very good advice. Then I asked him about certain other problems with the staging, especially the scene with the human sacrifices, which is very short, it's just a tableau, and lasts about two minutes in all. He said, "You know, you can suggest that, even by having priests go across the stage with knives and that sort of thing." Well, that wasn't enough, because there was much more than that involved, so I concocted that second tableau in the second act myself.

There was a big scene which went off in another direction in Borgese's text. I decided that that scene plus the first scene of the third act brings that problem in relief. The Spanish were horrified by the human sacrifices, which I understand very well, but that was a very solemn religious event for the Aztecs. But the Aztecs were similarly horrified by having two of their heroes burned at the stake in revenge and as punishment. Of course, the Spaniards called this an auto-da-fé, an act of faith, which carries the implication of a human sacrifice, too. It wasn't only the Spanish, but the Spanish made a big thing out of it, of course. And that had to be clear.

I assume that playwrights, like composers and everyone else creative, don't like to have things cut or tampered with, much less drastically cut.

Well, Borgese knew that it had to be cut. I told him about certain scenes which I had already cut out by that time. I said, "This scene simply can't go." And he said, "Oh that's a pity, because it's a very nice scene." That's a scene where the young Bernál isn't satisfied with the young Mexican woman who's been assigned to him, and so he goes to Montezuma and asks him if he can't have somebody else. Montezuma says, "Tell the daughter of the baker that she should call on the young man." Well, it's a cut scene, but the whole thing had to be condensed. And then the scene that I had written that I was going to play for Borgese was a scene after the battle, where there's a soldier who's bleeding to death on the battle-field. Cortez and the priest came in. It had to be cut. It was a grim story.

I had composed most of the music by 1959. I had to make a vocal score, but in order to make a vocal score, I had to make a particell first, which is a sort of condensed score with indications of what I'm going to do in the orchestra in many parts. And so I made a vocal score. That was immediately copied and printed for the singers.

Then I made the orchestral score, and that took me a year and three months—fifteen months. The vocal score was finished on July 1, 1962, and the orchestral score was finished on October 15, 1963, at 1 P.M. I put the time in there.

The production took place the following April. It was arranged maybe two years beforehand. The Berlin opera wanted to perform an American opera and asked the

State Department what American opera would be possible. They got word of *Montezuma* some way.

There was a lot of opposition in the Berlin press. I knew beforehand that they were going to do their best to make it a fiasco. They didn't really succeed in doing that. Half the audience was cheering and half the audience was booing. Sarah Caldwell and her mother were there, and her mother got into a fist fight: The man next to her was booing and she hit him. But we had a very good time backstage.

The press was against all contemporary opera because they had to pay taxes for it. They didn't get any money from the West Berlin government, you see. And West Berlin was inhabited by a large number of retired people and naturally young men escaping military service in West Germany. It was a funny place, a very funny place. People were against their producing an opera like this, because they would want to go hear *La Bohème* and they found it all sold out. They'd find that when *Moses and Aron* or *Montezuma* or something like that was playing, it wasn't sold out at all—plenty of seats.

How many performances did it receive?

I think there were four. It's a very hard thing to produce, because it's got such a big cast. If you're going to have good singers, you've got to schedule it at a time when they're all free to come.

Was it after the Berlin performance that Sarah Caldwell got the notion to produce this some day?

Yes. She had lunch with me a couple of days after the first performance, and she said she thought it was a lousy production. I wasn't quite ready to say that, because it was still going on. But she was rather scandalized by the production. And it took me a long time to realize how bad it actually was, as a matter of fact.

Cortez was the best of them, although his part lay a little too high for him. As a matter of fact, it did lie very high for a baritone, so I changed the vocal line. I did it for him, but I thought this was a good idea, because I got excited when I was writing it and . . . So of the five main singers Cortez was certainly the best; that was William Dooley, but he was sort of mildly hostile. Alvarado sang very well, but he had a little high-pitched voice. It was all right. The assistant conductor was sort of my ally through the whole thing, and he seemed to understand a little better than Hollreiser did, certainly better than Sellner, the director of the opera. He simply knew nothing about music, and I've never understood why they got a man of the prose theater who was used to putting on productions of Schiller, and I suppose Goethe, maybe an occasional Shakespeare performance, to head the opera house. The text and the music didn't even fit. I heard that during these vocal rehearsals, you simply didn't hear the musical line at all. I remember thinking to myself that next time it's performed maybe I'll hear it the way it should be.

And of course, the Berlin opera orchestra was not a good orchestra. I was astounded what a poor orchestra it was. I mean the violin section, the first stand men were fine, no problems at all. What went on in the second, third, fourth, fifth, sixth, and seventh stands, God knows. And the trombones were lousy, the trumpets were so-so. The horns were good, and so on. That's still a very sore spot with me.

To hear Sarah Caldwell's cast, to hear this music sound like music, was really quite an astonishing sensation.

Opera is an expensive venture anyway. I still am not quite sure what the plot of *Don Carlo* of Verdi is. You can more or less find it. One has to get over preconceptions about *the* opera. Opera has been so many different things.

The drama of *Montezuma* is the conflict between Europe and America, if you like, and also between the hawks and the doves, if you want to call them that, although they're not exactly dovelike, but they're intelligent people. Cortez isn't a nice man exactly; he's a warrior, but he's also an intelligent man. At least this is Bernál's book—nobody knows what he's really like aside from that.

You mentioned the Aztec words that are used in Montezuma.

Borgese put them down in English. Nahuatl is the name of the Aztec language. I was told that there was a man in the Metropolitan Museum who knew somebody who knew a lot about the Nahuatl language. I wrote to him and I sent him the text; he was very, very nice. He not only sent me the words, but he sent me a tape (which unfortunately I left in Berlin, but I think I remember it pretty well) with the pronunciations.

Some of the pronunciations are in the score, in fact.

In the first act, where the Aztec ambassador cries out, "Is he in his senses?!" I found two Nahuatl words I wanted, which would convey that. ["Tlaueliloc! Xolopi-tli!"] I went to the Princeton library, where they have all sorts of dictionaries. They don't have a Nahuatl dictionary, but they have a sort of treatise where you could find the words. That's up on the top floor. And the Spanish dictionaries are down in the basement. So I shuttled back and forth, and I found two words which I thought were right. Then I sent the score to this man in California and said I did the best I could. He wrote me back, "But you've got just exactly the right words."

In the first act, there's a translator who translates for Cortez some of the Aztec. I take it that it's just an operatic convenience, or convention, to forgo that kind of thing for the rest of the opera.

Borgese thought that we made our point, so the characters went through the motions of whispering together.

Now what about the Spanish words themselves? Did Borgese write those?

Borgese wrote those.

Of course there's some Latin.

I studied Latin as a child. The Latin in the opera was a part of the Catholic liturgy.
As I was working on *Montezuma,* I discovered things

about the row. I worked a lot with simple trichords; groups of three, there are four groups of three in the row. And I changed the order of the groups of three sometimes, just as I do with the order of the hexachords. I formulated my ideas about the row, and the kind of liberties you can take. If you think of three, you can take liberties with each group. And then you can take liberties within the hexachords. You can take no liberties with one hexachord and use the other one very freely, and so forth. And the greatest liberty of all is just using the twelve tones very freely and shuffling them around.

If you work with trichords and tetrachords, does that in some way help slow down the spilling out of all twelve pitches?

It makes things easier to organize, that's all. And it gave me guidelines by which I could attain the kind of organization that I wanted more readily and easily. And then, of course, I discovered resources just from using it. It's the way one's technique develops really.

I was thinking of Montezuma *as a kind of demarcation line in your work.*

Mainly because of its size, and because of the time that I worked on it, and because of the energy I put into it. I wouldn't want to go much farther than that, because I'd have to do that very systematically and give it an awful lot of thought and take a lot of time, which I don't have. But I have thought about it somewhat.

For instance, I discovered taking these four tri-chords—if you number them 1, 2, 3, 4—and in the first measure all the notes are there. I wrote that first measure, conceived that idea, years before using the twelve-tone system. Then I found that actually I wanted all the notes to be different, so they were. That's the basis of the row. I found a certain inner form to that row. [See the example on page 132.] In the first measure, the first hexachord comes in the horns and bass clarinet—just a chord; the first trichord: F, E, and F$^\sharp$. The F is in the bass clarinet and the E and the F$^\sharp$ are in the horns. Then come the violins and violas with the second trichord. Then comes the third trichord in the horns and bass clarinet, and the fourth trichord is just two whole tones. Now, on that basis, if I take the notes in the horns and bass clarinet together, and then the notes in the violas and violins and put them together [trichords 1 and 3], I get a symmetrical row. If I take the first and fourth tri-chords, I get another symmetrical row. I've got four reg-ular forms of the row, two of them symmetrical rows. And I use that a lot in *Montezuma*.

When did you write the first measure with the symmetrical row?

I thought of it first one day while feeding the furnace when I lived on a place called Carter Road outside of Princeton. This was, I suppose, in 1936 or 1937. I'd already begun having ideas for *Montezuma* before the text. I knew how it was going to begin. It was going to begin with the old Bernál, who's sort of narrator, and this was associated with this figure. So when I write dramatic music, I visualize the situation. I visualize the character. And when I write the vocal music, I visualize how he would sing these lines. It wasn't a twelve-tone row in its original form. It was just an idea. And very often I have ideas for which I have the general shape in mind, but I can work on the notes. I've always done that from way, way, back——*The Black Maskers*. Not always that way; I mean, sometimes the notes come all ready-made. But you make changes. That's what sketches are about.

Psalm 140 was originally written for organ and voice.

But I had the orchestra always in mind. I mean, the organ is not a medium in which I feel comfortable, really.

You've said that before, but I assume that part of the commission was that it be written for an organ.

Yes, exactly. But I orchestrated it afterwards. It's been given with orchestra at least as many times as with organ. The orchestral version is the definitive one. This opening is an orchestral passage, really. I mean, you hear the notes on the organ, and an organist can make them sound quite nicely. But I've got to have accent—you can't make an accent on an organ. You've got to sort of fake it. I think of the piano and string quartet as such, but I never thought of the organ as a real instrument. It's just not my instrument, that's all.

One of the instruments I used in the orchestra was a heckelphone. I used it partly because of the E in measure 26. I wanted a tone somewhat like the English horn. But the E is the lowest note on the English horn, and it's impossible to play it very softly. In Boston they had a sort of bass oboe, but the player couldn't play that softly, either, so this E came out. And then in Dartmouth, where I heard it played, they gave it to the bassoon. It's the only thing to do.

What led you to this text?

They wanted a religious text. And the Princeton Theological Seminary is a Presbyterian institution. I'm *not* a Presbyterian at all: I'm a sort of Catholic fellow traveler, in a way. I was very upset by what was going on in the world. I wanted to find something that meant something to me. The first part of the Psalm is about Senator Goldwater. The last part is about Pope John. Pope John died the day I finished it, and I thought of him. I had planned to dedicate it to Mrs. Harsanyi, who has sung a lot of my vocal music—she's sung *Theocritus* several times. She's a beautiful singer with absolute pitch, which is a great help. But I was almost tempted to dedicate it to Pope John, because the notice of his death came out when I was writing the end of it.

The Princeton Theological Seminary is sort of the St.

Peters of Presbyterianism in the United States. At lunch with the head of the seminary I told him, "You know, I almost dedicated this to Pope John, but then I thought, among other things, that it would be rather strange if I wrote a piece for the Princeton Theological Seminary and dedicated it to the pope." He said, "Oh, we wouldn't have minded. We think Pope John and Martin Luther King are the two greatest men living."

I think it's a wonderful psalm, one of the most wonderful psalms. This was the first piece I wrote after finishing the music for *Montezuma,* and I hadn't finished the orchestration for *Montezuma.* And I feel that *Montezuma,* which is the biggest work I've ever written, had a very, very, strong influence on all the music I've written since.

> *Is there any way to define what the influence of* Montezuma *was on subsequent works? Whether there was a stylistic change that was identifiable?*

Certainly *Montezuma* is the longest and biggest of all my works. and it has a very colorful text and a very wide range of style. Now don't get style mixed up with styles, because style and styles are two different things. I'm all for style, but I'm against styles. This is the main thing. All those things have had an influence that I've been aware of without being able to define exactly. Instrumentally, for instance, I used the marimba for the first time. And I used it very much in my Fifth Symphony. That's just one example.

> *Would you say that possibly it was because of working with such a large medium with so many different emotions and texts and such a large orchestra?*

Not only that, but there's a kind of exoticism in it. It's my own exoticism. I wasn't trying to write Mexican music, because there isn't any from that period. Although after writing *Montezuma*, I got acquainted with the music of Revueltas, and then I found there were certain resemblances between my Aztecs and his Aztecs, which interested me very much. I felt that my vocabulary had grown wider.

After the second of the Three Choruses on Biblical Texts, having to do with sin, the third piece is such an elevation of feeling. It seems to wash clean what has gone before it, as a kind of purifying element.

Sort of a general amnesty. In the texts I eliminated everything that referred to Israel, not for political reasons at all, obviously, but these are general sentiments, they're not applied to any one locality. Those other references didn't seem to me to be particularly relevant to musical treatment.

In the first one nothing is omitted except the last two verses, which are very specific religious references. And in the second one, I just took the verses that appealed to me. They seemed to go together. They're in the first two chapters of Isaiah, but there's an awful lot in there. He talks about the bad state of affairs locally. That's the Watergate one. Not only Watergate, but Vietnam, and so on.

I've always used the King James version, a wonderful work of literature. I don't think I changed the wording in the last one. The last three psalms are all "Praise ye the Lord," and they're all a little repetitive. I always call that my ecological psalm. It's the whole of nature, including human nature.

4

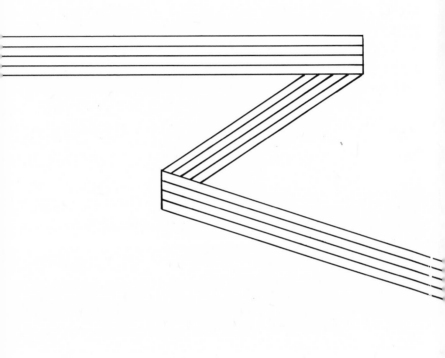

Biography

Tell me about your family.

Of course, I was born in Brooklyn. It was December 28, 1896, to be exact. Brooklyn at that time was a little like Westchester County is now. In the first place, it was a city that wasn't a borough of New York City. It became one when I was about two years old.

My father was a lawyer, and his father was a lawyer. In a way, he went into the law partly because his father wanted him to. I don't know exactly why he got out of it after his father died. My father was interested in politics. He ran for office. Also, he was a very devoted admirer of Grover Cleveland. It was the post–Civil War period, and my father hated Theodore Roosevelt, mainly because they had known each other at Harvard. In the 1884 presidential campaign the Republicans put up a crook. Everybody knew he was a thoroughly dishonest man. And the Democrats put up Grover Cleveland, who was certainly a very honest man and an intelligent man, and a lot of the Republicans switched over. They were called the Mugwumps.

My mother was the daughter of a bishop. My grandfather was bishop of Central New York. We're all, both my mother and my father, very old New England stock. I don't know that any of my ancestors came to this country after 1637. That's not true of my descendants. My wife's father was Dutch. That is, my second wife. Her mother was a curious mixture of Louisiana and Maine. But I'm talking of my own mother and father. I had an older sister who died some years ago and a younger brother who died.

We have an old, old family house in Hadley, Massachusetts, right on the Connecticut River. It's a wonderful old house. One of my ancestors was one of the founders of Hadley. In 1752 Moses Porter decided it was safe to build a house outside the town stockade. Sometimes it was subject to attack by the Indians, even by the French from Canada. Porter was a captain in the British army. He built this house outside the stockade in 1752 and went there with his wife, and they had a daughter. Then he had to go away to the Seven Years' War, which was called the French and Indian War. She was alone in the house with her daughter.

The Indians around there were friendly. One day she was knitting in a room on the ground floor, and there was a knock on the window and there was an Indian out there. He handed her her husband's sword, his spurs, and all the letters she had written him, which he'd never received. He'd been killed in New York State around Lake George.

Forty Acres is haunted, you know. Very strange things have happened there. There's even a secret passage. I love it very much, and I feel like one of the trees there.

That daughter was a remarkable person. She kept a diary for years—quite an interesting document. And eventually she married the richest man in the region and they had one daughter, too. Her name was the same, Elizabeth Phelps. She inherited this property and married a clergyman and professor at Yale. He moved up to Hadley, and they proceeded to have thirteen children, of whom the eldest was a daughter, again named Elizabeth, who was, I think, eighteen years older than her youngest brother. Now, this is very complicated: The oldest daughter was my father's grandmother and the youngest son was my mother's father.

I remember my grandfather. He died when I was seven years old. He became bishop of Central New York.

First he was a Unitarian minister. He became a professor of Christian Knowledge at Harvard. Then he got bored, so to speak, with the Unitarian church, and joined the Episcopal church and became a minister in Boston, and then became bishop of Central New York. I remember him. It amuses me to know that I know at least one person, and several others, who were born at a time when Beethoven was the greatest living composer and James Monroe was president of the United States.

He married a wonderful lady from Boston. I always told people I had a grandmother complex. She was descended from a man who was a general in the revolutionary war.

My mother as a young girl was very musical. She was born in Cambridge. In 1900 my father wanted to get out of the law, and he became the editor of a magazine. My younger brother was very, very ill, and my mother, I think in order to help him out, moved up to Massachusetts. She ran a house at Smith College, which is now named Sessions House.

I was very devoted to my father. They didn't really separate, but he lived in New York and she lived in Northampton. He came up and visited us from time to time. I don't know what went on, it was always a puzzle; it didn't simplify life for the children. I have come to this conclusion: I'm sure my mother was passionately in love with my father. And when they left each other, it was very different from what it was after two or three years. I think they both enjoyed their independence.

My father had three sisters; two were older and one was younger. One of them started out as a professional singer. She and my father too were very, very great friends of the family of the man who, in New York at that time, was conducting the Philharmonic—Theodore

Thomas. He did a tremendous amount for music in the second half of the nineteenth century. Thomas came over, I think, in 1848, and he played chamber music as a violinist. He introduced the great works of the nineteenth century. He played the Ninth Symphony of Beethoven for the first time in the United States. He played all the works of Wagner. My father knew him too. My father sang in the chorus. My aunt was a soloist. She couldn't stand it—she got so scared every time she sang that she couldn't endure it any more and gave it up.

My mother took piano lessons as a girl in Syracuse. She studied with an old German who was a very good musician. She had a Polish friend who thought she ought to go to Europe to study. She studied at the Leipzig Conservatory for two years. She had a royally good time, but she felt that they weren't really interested in her, and she didn't get her certificate, and she left. But she kept up her piano, so I heard music always in the house. Some very good music. I took piano lessons when I was four.

There were some rather nice little things in my *Lancelot and Elaine* which I wrote as a child and which I still remember with a certain, well, nostalgia, if you like. My mother, in her book, makes it much too complicated. The Guinevere melody has a resemblance to a motive in *Die Meistersinger.* And it wasn't well written, because I didn't know much about counterpoint. She doesn't sing the melody; it's in the accompaniment.

I went to boarding school in Newport, Rhode Island, for three months and that was *not* a good experience at all, although I think in the long run it had a very good effect, which was different from the one they wanted to produce. They wanted to produce good little boys who were ready to take their place in the very straitlaced society of that day. It's appalling. It was a very bad imitation of the English schools that you read about in *Tom Jones*. The motto that we were always taught: "Prompt and silent obedience is the first duty of the schoolboy and the soldier." My parents were appalled when I told them that, and they took me out at Christmas time.

I used to go to the piano and play little things. And then I went to this other school down in Essex Falls, New Jersey, a suburb of Newark. I was so much happier there than I was at Cloyne. I was thoroughly unhappy at Cloyne—there wasn't *anything* that I remember with pleasure. The older boys were encouraged to bully the younger boys and so forth. It was an awful place, but I think it taught me to be very tough later about such things. But it took a long time.

Anyway, I didn't do much with music. But then I came home in the summer of 1908. It was a *very* important year for me, because among other things, I had to have an appendicitis operation and was laid up at the end. But I took up music again. That fall I went to Kent School. I realized by that time that music was more important to me than anything else. I was eleven years old by that time.

In my Harvard lectures[1] published a few years ago, I mentioned that I had first encountered Schoenberg's music in 1912 when I was a sophomore in college. And when the book was reviewed, the reviewer said that my memory must be at fault, because how could I have known any Schoenberg in 1912? The answer is extremely simple. I used to go into Boston and buy all the music I could. I had heard the name Schoenberg—he was a "wild man" in those days. Always on the counter there was a pile of the latest publications in piano music. And

I found these Three Piano Pieces op. 11 by Arnold Schoenberg, so I bought it and took it home and sat down at the piano and played it. That's the way people got to know music. Everybody had a piano. In every house in Northampton there was a piano and somebody played. On the piano would be selections from operas. There would be easy sonatas by Haydn, perhaps, easy pieces of Chopin. Nocturnes and waltzes and that sort of thing. Sometimes more difficult pieces, too, and a lot of four-hand music. I played a great deal of music for four hands with my mother. That seems to me to be a rather important fact, also, because although they had gramophones in those days—but God help us if we had to listen to them—there were no so-called classical records. The first one that was really very good was made in 1917, and then they gradually began to appear.

In any case, there and when I was in college it was perfectly natural for students, even if they weren't music majors or anything like that, to have piano music around: arrangements of orchestral works. People got interested and got to know some contemporary music that way. My mother had some pieces by Debussy. My father would send around music from New York, and he had pieces by Debussy. This was somewhere around 1906–7–8. And early pieces by Richard Strauss. These were very contemporary composers at that time.

I remember walking once in Cambridge, and there was a man there who loved music. He was a fairly wealthy man, I guess. He used to invite people over to spend the evening playing and listening to music. I met him on the street one day. It must have been 1913 or 14. He stopped me on the street and said, "Have you seen those new waltzes of Ravel's?" and I said, "No." He didn't say, "Have you heard them?" he said, "Have you *seen* them?" He said, "Well, they're rather fascinating, but I can't quite make them out."

I can't imagine things like that happening nowadays at all, nor going into a music store and finding piano music by everybody under the sun, young people as well as established people, right on the counter. Nowadays, if you want something like that, you go to the store and they have to go look in the bottom drawer way over there somewhere, and maybe they have it and maybe they don't. You see what a different milieu it was.

How do you feel about your mother's book, Sixty-Odd?[2]

It's a book about herself. Don't believe anything about me. The point is that I went to boarding school and was away from home every winter from the age of nine. My mother was a very remarkable woman. I won't say disturbed, exactly; that's exaggerated, because the word "disturbed" carries a kind of psychiatric connotation; but she was, oh, very proud of being the daughter of a bishop and belonging to a very old New England family on the one hand, and very liberal on the other hand.

But liberal in the sense of charity rather than real recognition of human equality. She was very kind to everybody. When I came home from school and spoke of "niggers," she hit the ceiling, so to speak. Of course, she explained to me why; after all, I was nine or ten. She treated people as equals in their presence, but in the privacy of the home she didn't. You could see that wasn't her attitude.

This was very strange. I used to say all ladies were in love with their fathers at that time. And of course when the father was a *bishop,* he was the old man of the tribe. My mother and I had our differences. I didn't know how to deal with her, except I did learn gradually. She would burst out at me. When I learned to take it absolutely quietly and not fight back at all, but just keep my own counsel, then she would be shattered with remorse. Eventually, toward the end of her life, I thought, "She wants to be treated like a woman," and we got along beautifully at the end of her life.

She was a very jealous woman, and my younger brother was her favorite, and that really wrecked his life. She was very fond of my second wife. I *think* she was fond of my first wife in the beginning, but less so as time went on.

In the book I'm as she would have liked me to be. She was always afraid I was too serious about my music. She wanted me to entertain her guests by playing the piano, and I *hated* that. And I always wanted to play something that *I* liked, but she wanted me to play these darling little pieces that the guests liked. She herself knew much better, but she was living the social life of the world. I was always thoroughly rebellious. As far as the children were concerned, my older sister and my brother and I— they're all her rosy dreams in the book.

My mother's sisters were my maiden aunts who also lived there. Once when I brought home my friend Quincy Porter, my aunts talked with him from behind a screen. They decided Elizabeth Porter five generations back was their common ancestor, so Quincy Porter and I were fifth cousins. That kind of snobbish interest in family ancestors is oppressive, stifling, and dreadful. I don't like the text of *Forty Acres*[3] very much. There's an awful lot of Huntington family pride in there, and that always bored me very much.

I've run across that in my career, because my music was supposed to be very New England and so forth and austere. Of course, it's just the opposite. I don't think anybody who has ever known me has thought I was conspicuously austere. But it is true that Boston society at that time was somewhat of a closed society.

What about your Harvard years?

When I was in college, I spent most of my time reading and going to concerts. Every now and then I'd go to class. And sometimes, especially toward the exams, I'd do some studying. I read all sorts of things when I was in college. I read all the plays of Ibsen, didn't understand a word of them of course, but I thought they were wonderful. They had an elective system, not too much for a boy of fourteen. My college career wasn't well planned. A curious thing happened, a sort of academic mixup. They had a very stuffy dean of students there. His name was Parker, and he was affectionately termed by the students "C+ Parker" because he never gave anything higher than a C+. It was sort of like the income tax now; you made a preliminary plan of courses in the spring and then you finished it in the fall. I was always in the habit of undertaking much more than I could do. And I was trying to keep this magazine the *Harvard Musical Review* going. I'm still not a very good planner of things. I found that I had an awful lot of work to do myself.

I was taking a chemistry course. I'd taken an elemen-

tary chemistry course and I'd rather liked it, so I decided
to take another course. And this course was not my kind
of course at all. It was a course in qualitative analysis.
We were told to clean out our little dishes with hydrochloric acid. I was in a hurry one day, and I thought I
might help things along if I added some sulphuric acid
too. The sulphuric acid absorbs all the water, so the
clouds of hydrochloric acid and smoke kept coming
along. And finally some students came and took me by
the arms and rushed me to the window. And I was all
right. And I was terribly tempted by the pot of cyanide
of potassium. I wanted to smell it to see what it was
really like, but luckily I didn't quite dare.

OK, I flunked the chemistry course. I had too many
courses. I was taking a psychology course, but I wanted
to drop chemistry and keep on with the psychology, because I had too many courses, more courses than were
required. So I went to C + Parker, and he refused. He
said, "You can drop this psychology course." (It's fun to
remember.) I had written a thesis on some musical
acoustics. I wrote a paper called "The Psychological Basis of Modern Dissonance."[4] This was in 1914; of course,
it's way out of date now. But it talked about the *Sacre du
Printemps* and *Elektra.*

So I had to go back to summer school to get my degree. I looked naively at the summer school schedule.
I thought, "Well, I suppose I should take a science course
to make up for the chemistry." But the course that really
interested me was a course in military history, not so
much because of the First World War, which was going
on, but because of the Civil War. I started out by taking
a botany course, but there was only one other student
who applied for the botany course, so it was dropped
and I was very happy. I thought, "I can be free to take

the military history course" and I took that and passed it with flying colors. I could have told you after that course every time General Grant lit his cigar during the Battle of the Wilderness. And just how they moved around the battlefield of Spottsylvania.

Anyway, I got my degree. Then in that fall I went to Yale, and one day I was walking across the campus and I met the young instructor who was the assistant in the psychology course. We got to know each other very well, went around a lot. With another man we called ourselves "the Trinity." The psychology man was God the Father, and the literature professor was God the Son, and I was the Holy Ghost. (I hope that doesn't seem irreverent to you. It was, slightly. I don't think God minded.)

Anyway he asked me one day, "Why did you drop that psychology course? You know you were getting straight As." And I told him what happened. He said, "Well you wouldn't have had to do well in the exam, you'd passed it with flying colors anyway."

When I got an honorary degree from Harvard years later, I was sitting up there and thought to myself, "I wonder if they looked at my academic record?" [laughter]

What did you do during the war?

In the first place, my oculist was chairman of the draft board. I was against the war at the beginning. My mother was a violent pacifist, although she wanted the Allies to win—it wasn't very consistent of her. She even got furious when I decided that I *wasn't* against the war. She said I was betraying her. She had lived in Germany and was very anti-German, and of course there was a terrific spy hysteria during that time. It was a lot of nonsense. The United States was much more naive and gullible than it is now. It's still gullible on the subject of Communism, of course.

But I thought, "Since I want the Allies to win, I ought to try to go." I was much more involved than a lot of people who were drafted and did go. So I went to my oculist and said, "Tell me what are the requirements for eyes in other countries?" He looked them up, and he said, "The only army you could get into would be the French army." But then I found that it was, of course, impossible to get into any army during wartime except the American army. My sister was married to a colonel in the army; he was an officer of some kind. He volunteered. He said I couldn't possibly get into any other army because it was against the law, so I didn't pursue the matter further. That's what really happened. I did work at Fort Devens in Ayer, Massachusetts, for the summer of 1918. We didn't get into the war until 1917, and by that time I was twenty. The war ended the following November.

For the Second World War I was overage; I was just forty-five. There was no question of my going. I became an air-raid warden in Princeton in the Second World War. When they didn't have air-raid wardens any more, I joined the Princeton emergency police force.

You chose to live in Berlin, rather than Paris, in the thirties.

Florence is the Italian city I like best. I mean Rome always seemed to have something vaguely second-rate about it, except for the Vatican, of course. They've got a very good pope now, I think [John Paul II]. They're still against abortion. The pope is very important. Because after all, the Catholic church really created Europe. They kept the kings, who were always fighting each other, in some kind of order.

Berlin was by far the most exciting place then. Of course, the people I knew in France, Nadia Boulanger in particular, never forgave me for moving there. But as far as musical life goes, that was the high point of my whole life. The main reason was because of Klemperer, whom I met when he was conducting in Rome. In Rome, when a visiting conductor comes, they don't give parties all over the place as they do here. So I saw a lot of him; we went on walks together and had meals together. He urged me to come to Berlin. I went to Berlin, and he threw the musical doors open to me. Anytime I wanted to go to the opera, I just had to call him up to get tickets. I didn't pay for a single ticket while I was in Berlin. He introduced me to other people—Schnabel, whom I came to know even better, but more in the United States.

I met everybody in Berlin. I went to concerts every night, practically. There was just one thing I missed: a performance of Weber's *Euryanthe,* which I've loved since I was sixteen years old. I never heard a live performance. Now, of course, it's suddenly blossoming, because there are these new records. Everybody's discovering what a wonderful work it is. It's historically very important. I always used to say it's the greatest of Wagner's early works. But it's got a very complicated libretto, and that's been a handicap to it in the opera houses, because nobody can quite tell what's going on. But it's a marvelous work. Now the records have come out, and everybody is discovering it and raving about this work. So it's almost a personal triumph, in a way.

You once mentioned that you knew journalists in Berlin.

That was during the last year I was there, the year Hitler came to power. I had a friend who was a correspondent for one of the London papers, the *London Morning Post,* which was actually a very conservative paper, but a very good paper in London. He took me to the cafe table where all the foreign correspondents met every night. There were people from Brazil there. So I had a front seat to the rather awful political things that were going on in Germany at that time. I became very aware of things. And when I came back to this country, nobody would believe anything I said. If they had, a lot of people would be alive today that are not. I don't mean that I would have saved them at all, but simply that it took this country a long time before they realized what was going on. Even then they were slow about it.

I was there from 1931 to 1933. We had an apartment, and I rented a studio about a block away. This was owned by a formerly very rich Jewish family who had lost all their money in the inflation of 1922, and they had to rent rooms. I saw something of them; I liked them. They, like everybody else in Berlin, talked about practically nothing but politics all the time. So I got a lot of information from them.

Also, I had a cousin-in-law who was in the nickel business in Berlin. He thought I was very lucky, "being an artist and not a businessman, because you're not affected by all this." That was nonsense. He was affected more dramatically, because he lost more money than

I did in marks. After Hitler came to power, he said to me, "I congratulate you for not being a businessman, but I congratulate you even more for not being a German." He was absolutely horrified. A couple of years later he had to give in, as so many Jews did. People over here had *no* idea, and still people have no idea what was going on, what it was really like.

The young man in the Jewish family from whom I rented my studio was a very successful lawyer in Berlin. He had a friend who visited him quite often from Vienna. And I thought that Hitler had been disposed of, because there was an election in November 1932 in which Hitler's vote went way, way down. This man from Vienna and I were talking about the situation. I said, "Hitler is disposed of now, isn't he?" And he said, "Oh, no, no. Hitler will be chancellor. But don't worry about it, because he's not going to do anything the way he talks." Well, I'd lived in Italy for six years under Mussolini. I said, "No, I don't agree at all, because I lived under Mussolini, and if he gets into power, it'll be just as he says." He said, "Oh, no, don't worry."

Well, being an American, I was wrong about the electoral process in Germany. And this was different from the present, alas. But I was right about Hitler. Three weeks after Hitler came into power, this young man in this family couldn't practice law any more. Bruno Walter couldn't conduct in Germany any more. Men I knew who were connected with the opera lost their jobs. Klemperer, a very great conductor, was an idiot in some ways about politics. Klemperer was sent over to the other opera, where he had to share the top with Furt-wängler and Bruno Walter. So when Hitler abolished the Prussian government, he was delighted. But then, suddenly, he woke up and took the fastest train that he could for Italy. I saw him in Florence some months later. He was as violently anti-Hitler then—he was a violent man—as he had been pro-Hitler in Berlin.

One day the Jews were all boycotted. With my friend from the British press, we all ostentatiously went into a Jewish restaurant and were photographed as we were going in there. But they wanted to keep in well with the press at that time, so we didn't feel personally endangered by it at all. It had been an artistic tradition in Germany that artists had nothing to do with politics. It worked very well until a situation like that came up.

When I got back to Princeton, my friends said, "Our children went over to Germany and they had a wonderful time. Everything is fine over there." These were decent, very liberal people.

In the thirties you didn't write as much music every year as you've written since that time.

In the first place, this was the worst period of my life. I felt totally alone, because I was entirely opposite the current that was going around here. I was just back from Europe, where I had a wonderful time.

I had gotten my divorce, which is *always* a trauma and a bad situation, as my first wife said before we got it. We both wanted it and we were friendly. But one realized that one is not divorcing simply a human being, one is divorcing one's home and one's whole life. And nobody ever knows the inside story of these things, and some people don't understand and take violent sides, and others *do* understand and accept the situation.

Also the business about the cancelation of the premiere of my Violin Concerto was a disaster, because

Spalding had made so much publicity about it ahead of time. And the word went around that the concerto was unplayable, and that it wasn't finished even, when it was even published about two weeks after the date set for the first performance. If it hadn't been for some wonderful friends I had, like Schnabel and Klemperer and others, it would have been a desperate situation.

I had been living in Europe on fellowships, so I had to get a job. I taught privately; I had a lot of pupils, but the ones who could pay were very slow about paying me, and I finally had to appeal to the ones who really didn't have much money, and they gave me endorsed checks because they were concerned.

I was at Princeton by the time I remarried, but on a very low salary, because the music department was living on a shoestring and the head of the department had to raise all the money. I got the salary of lecturer with the rank of associate professor. It meant that I didn't have tenure. I found out they weren't trying to get rid of me. I thought at first they were. Those years were awful years, really.

I had no friends really among American musicians at all. Also, I had to work very hard at Princeton like any younger member of the faculty. I also had a job at what they called New Jersey College for Women then (it's now Douglass College), and I traveled twice a week from Princeton to New Brunswick. It isn't very far, but it took a lot of time, and so I composed very little. Those years between 1935 and 1940 were very tough years, that's all.

You returned to Europe in the early fifties.

When I had a Fulbright in 1951, I gave lectures on American music. I played something by Copland and

Roy Harris's Third Symphony (a piece I don't like very much). I lectured all over Italy, from Naples to Savona, Genoa, and Turin, and Allesandria, Milano, and Venice. That little book *Reflections on the Music Life in the United States*[5] is the lectures I gave in Florence. I gave all the lectures in Italian.

I want to tell you what really happened with *Reflections on the Music Life in the United States.* I had given these lectures in Florence in Italian. If one speaks another language really quite well, it's very, very hard to translate what one's said in one language into another one. It's awfully hard. Then pressure was applied to me; I shouldn't have given in. This German musicologist wanted a book for a series that was being published in English. I thought, "Why don't I just quickly translate these lectures I gave in Florence?" So I told him I'd do that.

But I put it off and I put it off. Then I got a letter from a lawyer threatening me with a suit for breach of contract; I should have taken it to my own lawyer, but it would have cost more. We were about to go abroad. I told him, "I'll send you a translation. I'll sit down and work on it very hard." I knew I could do it quickly, and I did. I must say that I know how to write; I am not an illiterate writer of English.

I sent it off and gave the musicologist my address and the dates where and when I would be in Europe. No proofs arrived. I wasn't too concerned, because I hadn't wanted to do this thing, anyway. Instead of proofs, nine copies of the finished volume appeared. Even the title is not English at all: we don't say "the music life." It's good German: *Das Musikleben.* I thought, "My God!" Then I looked inside the book. I start out by telling a little of my experiences, how I went to study with Bloch, how I told my parents I was going to be a composer. I found "we told our parents" and "we went to Ernest Bloch." It was clumsy English. I thought, "My God, what happened?" I found sentences which I'd written that were very clear in the original: I'd written: "A real composer has only one choice and that is to be himself. The only alternative is not being anybody." I hope that is clear. It means simply that the music becomes completely neutral unless there's a lot of juice behind it. That sentence was so distorted.

That's why I so to speak put the book in the waste basket and disowned it. Another friend of mine connected with a big publishing company scolded me and said, "You could perfectly well have forced them to withdraw the book from the market." I said I was awfully busy writing a big work and I didn't want to get involved with legal things at that point, because I didn't have the time. That was what happened. I made the original translation; it was the bowdlerizing of my translation that was the problem.

What prompted you to leave Princeton and go to California?

In the first place, I was sick of Princeton. Secondly, in universities they don't see creative work as serious accomplishment from their point of view. I found that my musicological colleague Oliver Strunk could have all the room he wanted, but I couldn't have a room where I could go and work. I didn't like that; and also the situation in Princeton then was that the head of the department had to go and raise all the money. I made up my mind and said, "I want to go to California." They said, "What would you want Princeton to be like if you stayed here?" I told them, "In the first place the money would have to come out of the university budget instead of having to have the chairman go out and raise all the money." We were a part of the Department of Fine Arts, Architecture, and Music. He told me that that *was* fixed up before I left.

I've *never* been comfortable on a university faculty. There've always been problems. The Princeton musicologists thought of the music department as their private domain, and composers should be second-class citizens; well, I never was a second-class citizen in California.

You got along with Oliver Strunk, I gather, even though he had more room.

Well, during the war there was talk of one of the two of us resigning, and he said, "I think for the department it would be better if you resign." I said, "Well, Oliver, I'm sorry, but I've got tenure, and you haven't got tenure. Furthermore, I've got children, and you don't have children, so I'm not going to resign." His face fell. Neither of us had to resign, and we were very good friends always, still are.

Was it during this time, 1944–1945, that you worked together on the translation of Einstein's The Italian Madrigal?[6]

Yes. I worked on it, but he took over and did the final version. I got the Princeton University Press to publish it, and then I shopped around for a translator, and we got a man who was highly recommended to us by the head of the Italian department. This man was strangeness itself; he did an absolutely disgraceful job. I did the best I could in sort of cleaning it up a little bit. I told Oliver to go over it; he found a lot of things to be corrected.

Where was Alfred Einstein during this?

He was up at Smith. I got him that job, too. He was a very, very lovely person. He was one of the good musicologists.

If you didn't like universities, you were sort of going from the fire to the frying pan, as it were, to go from Princeton to the University of California.

I'll tell you: California is a funny place, naturally, with individual exceptions. The exceptions being very largely people who were born in California and whose parents were born in California, the old families. The large majority of Californians then, as since, have been people who moved there from other parts of the country. It's rather strange. The point is that even the old people don't have the arrogance that the others do, but they have still the inferiority complex. It's a strange mixture of arrogance and inferiority complex.

I found that the first two years were the best. Bloch came to see me shortly after I went there. I'd been there a year. He said, "Tell me, how do you like it out here?" I said, "I think it's wonderful. I've never been in such a wonderful place as this." (I wasn't thinking of Florence then.) I meant the situation, the job and everything. And he said, "Yes, it is wonderful, of course. Of course, after a while you'll get to realize it's all a little *Ach wie flüchtig, Ach wie nichtig!*" That's the first line of a Bach chorale [BWV 26] which means, "Oh, how fleeting, oh, how insignificant." [laughter]

You were describing telling Bloch how much you liked your job there. What kind of job was it?

I was a professor in the music department. One of the things that made me make the decision to move was that they said that my creative work was really important to them, and they wanted to plan my schedule so that it would favor that as much as possible. And they did. It was a quite different attitude from the attitude at Princeton.

It was a very nice place to teach because everybody liked each other.

But you did ultimately have problems at the University of California. With Albert Elkus as chairman, I gather everything was fine, but when Nin-Culmell became chairman, there were problems. I remember you and I met him one day here at Juilliard.

He really wrecked the department the minute he became chairman. As a visiting professor he seemed very nice and able to get along with everybody, but then the minute he became chairman, he took over. He was a rather weak man, and he leaned on people and then would throw them over rapidly. It became impossible. The department was in a way disintegrating. The department had always been very harmonious until Albert Elkus retired in 1950, but then it exploded.

By 1951, when you went on a sabbatical with a Fulbright, were you ready to leave California?

Yes, I think so. I really wanted to get back east, because this is where I belong. It's near New York. See, I went out there partly because I felt that other parts of the country were *too* dependent on New York. I had had the feeling that something indigenous was getting started out there. That was a disappointment when I found how essentially provincial it was. And yet the university is a *very* impressive place; the whole university is very impressive. I would say that California and Harvard were the two really great universities in this country—but totally different.

We still have friends out there, the Imbries, and Alexander Meiklejohn, who died out there, also a man in the geology department.

Stravinsky and Schoenberg lived in California for a while. Did you see them there?

I saw Schoenberg in California always. You didn't go to see them both. I felt I was far away from Stravinsky musically at that time, although I always told people that in twenty-five years Stravinsky and Schoenberg would not seem to be at such opposite poles as they did. It's funny, because a couple of years later Stravinsky began using the twelve-tone system. They were both reacting in different ways to the same general musical situation in the world.

I didn't see Stravinsky when I was in California; I saw Stravinsky mostly after I was back here. I began seeing Stravinsky in about 1959.

You see, I didn't want to be in the retinue of either of these people. Schoenberg seemed really a greater musical personality than Stravinsky did. I don't lay much stress on that fact. I could talk very seriously with Schoenberg. I always had an awfully good time with Stravinsky, because he was a very warm, open person. He'd had a successful life and Schoenberg had had a very, very tough life, in Vienna especially. I was living in Princeton and Stravinsky was often in New York. The last time I saw Stravinsky was actually in California in 1968.

Every time I went to Los Angeles I called Schoenberg up. Only, the time in 1950, when I spent half the summer down in Los Angeles, I called him up, but he was too ill to see anybody then. But otherwise, I always saw him and went to his house.

The Schnitzlers had moved down to Los Angeles, and we visited them. They lent me one of their cars, and one evening I drove up to Schoenberg's and saw him. I found that Schoenberg had a driveway that you could drive into, but you had to back out. I teased him saying, "You ought to arrange it so that you could back out upside down, too." He was very much amused by that. I had a good time with Schoenberg, too, but we weren't simply joking. I wasn't simply joking with Stravinsky, either, but he was a different kind of personality, that's all.

I was friends with both Thomas Mann and with Schoenberg. I was the best man at the wedding between Mann's daughter and Borgese, the librettist for *Montezuma*. One Thanksgiving dinner with Schoenberg the topic of Thomas Mann came up. Schoenberg remarked that he was afraid that history would credit the invention of the twelve-tone method to a little-known German composer named Adrian Leverküln. I tried to reassure him tactfully; however, what was really going on in my mind was, "What do you care? You will be remembered for your *music,* not for inventing the twelve-tone system."

My friends Schnabel, Klemperer, Monteux, Casadesus were in a way my real sustenance. Naturally, Schoenberg was, and I think Stravinsky eventually—well, I know Stravinsky was. He was one of the nicest human beings in the world.

Once we were in California for the winter, and Stravinsky came to Princeton because he had a commission for the *Requiem Canticles* from a very rich ex-Princeton student from Texas. This student's mother had died, and he commissioned these from Stravinsky for that. Stravinsky was at a big reception, and my daughter Betsy was there. Nobody paid any attention to Betsy at all; they don't to one's children. Stravinsky asked where I was and was told I was in California. Stravinsky made them send Betsy in, and he talked to Betsy alone; he was awfully nice.

Another time there was a big concert of Stravinsky's music and a reception afterwards. I didn't go near Stravinsky; everybody was crowding around him. But then he was standing alone, waiting for a drink, so I went and stood next to him. We were interrupted by someone, and Stravinsky whispered in my ear, "I love you." I said, "Well, I love you, too."

I always had an awfully good time with him. We had arguments, but each one was saying the other one was right. Very good arguments. One of the very nice times I remember was when he told me all about his visit to the

Soviet Union. I got together with him just before I went to the Soviet Union [in 1958]. He greeted me at the door and said, "I've got a wonderful bottle of scotch." We sat down and drank scotch and talked about Russia a little. He told me about his trip to Russia; he told me about how they asked him about his relations with Schoenberg. They wanted to get some dirt on Schoenberg. Stravinsky said, "My relations with Schoenberg have no importance whatever. What has importance is that Schoenberg was one of the greatest artists of our time, and you'll have to recognize that in ten years, so why not start now?"

We went on; he told me about a new recording he had that was quite good. He said, "The orchestra isn't very good, but it's a very good recording and a good performance." I said, "Well, I don't like an orchestra to be too good." He sort of looked at me for a moment, wondering what I meant. I said, "Well, I like an orchestra where the oboe sounds like an oboe and the bassoon sounds like a bassoon—there's a little dirt in the sound." He brightened up and said, "I do too." [laughter]

> *Of course, he has the bassoon in the opening of the* Rite of Spring *sounding like some kind of strange instrument.*

Yes. Of course, Casella told me that story, which he got from Saint-Saëns, who started *his* career hearing Mendelssohn conduct. Ten years before he died he heard the *Sacre du Printemps*. Saint-Saëns came to Casella and said, "What instrument's that?" Casella said, "That's a bassoon." Saint-Saëns said, "It's not true," and got up and walked out of the hall.

Of course, that was in the days of Stokowski, who

was a remarkable personality. He was *not* such a great conductor, because he didn't always understand the music. He played a lot of contemporary music, but he didn't even give a very good performance of *The Black Maskers* with the Philadelphia Orchestra, which was at that time the best orchestra in the country. It sounded very well and it had success and all that sort of thing. They played Mozart's *Jupiter* Symphony and Handel's *Water Music*. The reason I didn't like it was because you couldn't tell the strings from the woodwinds. There was no real contrast—everything had a sort of shimmery sound. The whole point was, everything was sacrificed; the *Jupiter* Symphony was the worst horror on the program because there was no contrast, no depth in the orchestral sound. It was all this shimmery color, you see.

I had a little punch line myself some years ago, and that is, "Enough rehearsals are too many rehearsals." What it means is that if the players are totally sure of themselves, then they don't play so well as if they are a little nervous. I mean they don't put so much juice into it.

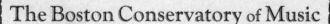

The Boston Conservatory of Music

Announces the Engagement of

ROGER SESSIONS

Distinguished American Composer

MR. SESSIONS WILL CONDUCT COURSES IN

THEORY OF COMPOSITION

(Harmony, Counterpoint, Instrumentation, Composition)

CLASSES NOW FORMING

for further information address the

Boston Conservatory of Music

KENmore 1574   256 Huntington Avenue, Boston

Brochure advertising Sessions's engagement with the Boston Conservatory of Music upon his return to the United States in 1933. Courtesy of the Boston Conservatory.

Roger Sessions, Leonard Bernstein, and Tossy Spivakovsky preparing for the 1959 performance of the Concerto for Violin and Orchestra. A Balakar– Cosmo photograph.

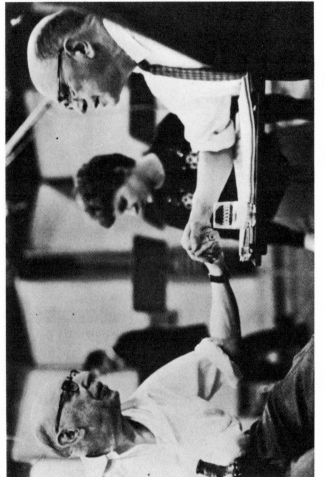

Igor Stravinsky and Roger Sessions in the early 1960s. From a BMI pamphlet on Roger Sessions.

177

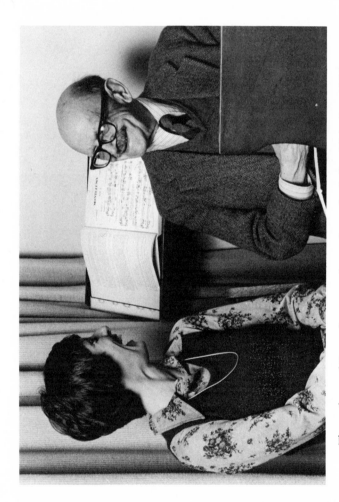

The author and Roger Sessions in his studio at the Juilliard School in 1976. Photograph by Stan Fellerman.

Roger Sessions at Juilliard in 1981. Photograph by Ellen Taaffe Zwilich.

Symphony No. 9, first movement, manuscript page.

Analysis and
Theory

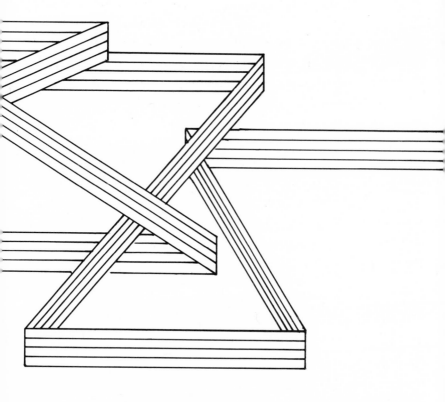

In my family my book *Harmonic Practice*[1] is known as "that God-damn book." That's what I called it. I thought it would take me about two months to write a harmony book, and so I agreed to do it. And then it took me two years, because I had to make up eight hundred exercises—over eight hundred exercises—and I found I could write a harmony book in two months or maybe even less, but it wouldn't be a harmony book by me.

The son of the textbook editor of Harcourt, Brace was a pupil of mine in Princeton. He thought I ought to write a harmony book. He got his father to press me into writing this. I didn't know what I was getting in for. And I finally consented. Then they did a very unnecessarily fancy job of printing it with wide margins, so that the student could make notes. That's all very well. I had a telephone call, and they wanted me to shorten it so they could keep the price under $5.00. And I said, "What suggestions have you got?" And they said, "Shorten the introduction." I said, "No. I can't shorten the introduction; that's the most important part of the book." And finally I said, "What's the alternative?" "The alternative would be to let us extend the time before you get full royalties." I got only a certain percentage. And I said, "By all means, that's what we do." So we did it. They sold it for five dollars and a quarter, five dollars and a half. This was in 1951. Now it's about $14.00 or something like that. But it stayed in print and I make about $1,000 a year or so.

I know a lot of people who have gone through harmony and have used this book.

If you go through that book and do all the exercises and do them well and carefully, then you know your harmony. That's the kind of book I wanted to write. You learn harmony by practice, not by doing ten exercises at the end of chapter one and having the teacher correct them and then going on to chapter two. You have to do it so that it's harder to make a mistake than it is to write it correctly.

I wrote eight hundred exercises for *Harmonic Practice*. I'd taken quote unquote harmony, and I found that I hadn't the mastery and the understanding that I wanted to have. Then Bloch lent me a little book by his teacher, who was a pupil of Brahms. He had several teachers, but this was the man he got the most from; it was a man named Ivan Knorr, who I think lived in Frankfurt. Knorr had written a little book which I thought was the ideal harmony book, because it was nothing but exercises. He had very slight directions; he took it for granted that one would know what to do if one were properly pre-pared. I was more or less disaffected with all the har-mony books that I'd seen in this country before. I thought, "This is the real thing." I did the exercises, and I got a lot out of them. That was the kind of book I planned.

So I wrote it, and then the trouble began. I sent it to the publisher. I didn't know this was going to happen, but he sent it to harmony teachers all over the country. They said that there were too many exercises and too little explanation. Explanation is a lot of words, generally, very standardized. So in a way my harmony book was a reaction against *that* kind of harmony teaching. He wrote me a letter and said, "Now you should really pitch in and do the text." [laughter] That was why that book became "that God-damned blank, blank, blank, blank, blank book." I had to pitch in and write explanations of the kind that *I* thought were necessary. And I wrote a long introduction explaining my point of view. I was amused by writing the exercises, but I was very bored by writing these explanations. I even thought, "To hell with the whole business!" But then I thought, "I worked on this for a whole year, so I might as well make some money out of it." I haven't looked at this thing for years, so I've forgotten what I wrote. It's been in circulation twenty-five years.

This story may be the reason why some other harmony teachers object to it.

Although not wholeheartedly. They loved the exercises; it's the prose that the critics found some troubles with, although overall the reviews that I read were positive.

Let me give you one example of the lengths to which this thing went. I was in Minneapolis for the premiere of my Fourth Symphony, and there was a young man who came in absolutely glowing after the performance. He said, "My God, they talk about Stravinsky's wonderful orchestration, why don't they talk about yours?" He was raving about my symphony.

And then there was a party afterwards; I don't remember all the details. But at the party he explained to me that I, like Mozart and other people, were wonderful instinctive composers, but we didn't really know what we were doing. We didn't know anything about music. This argument got really a little nasty. The conductor Dorati was on my side, and Seymour Shifrin was certainly on my side. This man said, "For instance, there are so many mistakes in your harmony book. For instance, you have a place where you have a G♯ going to a G natural and then to an F♯ and the E is held. And then the B below goes to a B♯ and then goes to a C♯. Now, why won't you admit that that's a C-major triad in there?" I said, "Well, it isn't. It's the result of two voices coming chromatically together."

That sort of comment is the result of the whole out-worn system of most harmony books that comes right out of the now-frozen teaching methods of the late nineteenth century, where everything is a chord and the main thing is to identify the chord but not to pay any attention to the context. That is part of the reason why a lot of people didn't like my harmony book, because it tried to clarify those things.

It's a little like another argument that I started. You remember Beethoven's first quartet [op. 18, no. 1]? [sings the opening] Very often people play [sings, putting an accent on the downbeat of the second measure]. The C and the D are the part that moves. The next measure has an E in the cello, the next measure has an F which brings in the cadence. Now I don't think it should be [sings again, accenting the downbeat of the second bar], but I think one should accent where the weight falls. I

think I said in that book: I don't mean that it should be accented, but it should be very solid.

And that reminds me of something else. You've heard me speak of Klemperer. Klemperer was a very remarkable man—I don't think there's ever been a human being like him. He was a sophisticated man, but he was an extremely primitive man, too. And there are all sorts of stories about him, because he had no inhibitions whatever. He was a devout Catholic as well as a Jew. He was absolutely absorbed in music. I was talking to Schnabel about Klemperer one day. He was a great friend of Schnabel's. I said, "You know, there's only one thing about Klemperer's conducting that I've never understood. It's the only thing that has bothered me sometimes. And that is that when he comes to the final chord, he's apt to cut it so short that you feel a little left up in the air there." Schnabel smiled and nodded and said, "Yes, I feel that, too."

That's what I was talking about. The end of the phrase is where you're going. It's got to be very definite there. Although I'd spent a page explaining that, nobody'd read what I'd written carefully enough to understand that I wasn't proposing [sings with a strong accent on the downbeat]. That's not it at all. In fact, I've often said, "The first beat of the measure is the one thing that doesn't need to be accented if it's played properly." Accent is in the upbeat; that's where the music is. It's got to end solidly, you see. But these sorts of things are so seldom noticed. You have harmony teachers who even write books sometimes, and they just don't understand music, that's all.

Why some people have called my terminology vague is because they're used to having very conventional terms. If I speak of *gesture,* I mean the whole shape of the phrase. [sings the Beethoven quartet again] That's certainly a gesture of a kind.

Music is inherently difficult to write about and you seem aware of that difficulty.

Very, very hard to write or talk about music accurately and know what you're talking about. I've really written more prose than I had any business to. Of course, I think most books about music are not worth the paper they're written on. It's very hard to write about music, that's the trouble. I read an article on Wagner the other day by Robert Craft. It wasn't very good, because it was, in a way, the same old stuff, you see. It had some awfully silly things in it, and it's probably simply because it's very hard to talk about these things.

We musicologists, of course, have to talk about music, and it's a difficult obstacle to overcome.

Of course, that's true, but in a way you have something a little more tangible to write about than really talking about music itself. And of course, it's *bound* to be somewhat subjective. Journalism and *real* musical criticism, in the sense of insight, are two different things, simply two different things.

Once I made a statement on an occasion—this must have been in the mid-thirties. There was a meeting in upper New York State, and I was there. Then some of my remarks were reported in the paper. And I was on the train with a critic from the *Herald Tribune*. I asked him if this could be corrected, because my remark was just distorted a little, not through anybody's fault. This man, whom I like very much, said, "You know, you shouldn't worry. Journalism is for the *day*." And it's true. It's what the word means.

The point is this, Andrea, that these technical terms that you know I object to are interpreted in so many different ways by different people. I point out about the word "theme"—people talk about a nice cantilena as the theme. It isn't the theme, there's no theme there, it's the melody, the principal voice. When you talk about a theme, what the word "theme" means is: What's it all about? So I called it "associative element" instead, something which is even more technical. Anything can be it: if I make a vocal gesture, let's say [sings a low note sliding to a high note]. Just that, regardless of notes, can be connected with other things. A gesture refers to the character of the melody. It's a word for the dynamic character a melody, or a fragment, may possess.

This business about filing cabinets; we all have filing cabinets. (I don't have the cabinet, but I have the folders.) I got quite depressed one time about how classifications stuck. It's very necessary to reexamine those classifications every now and then. I was thinking of that one day in California while walking to the university. I met a friend of mine who was in the English department. He asked me what I was thinking about, and I said, "I want to reform the whole Western culture." (I wasn't very serious.) He said, "You want to abolish Plato?" I thought a minute and said, "No, I think it's Aristotle I want to abolish." What I really mean is that one gets in the habit of making big categories.

For instance, you take the "Renaissance." People use that term as if the Renaissance began at a certain hour on a certain day and ended on a certain hour. A very dear friend of mine, a student of Benedetto Croce, was pointing out in some lectures that the Renaissance was a very slow process, you could take it back even to Dante in a certain sense, or to St. Francis. It was a big movement that took place over years. Then he got into a fight with a man who was a very orthodox Episcopalian, because he thought that when Raffaelo Piccoli talked about the Renaissance he was slighting the Middle Ages, which was his field.

I think the categories which are used so often very carelessly and very rigidly and certain names for things have gotten so awfully dog-eared and worn that I like to get something that's a little fresher, that's all. I don't object to filing cabinets; I just think that they should be emptied out and rearranged every now and then.

You write of my talking of "inspiration" in one book and then putting it a little differently in another book. That's because the word "inspiration" is used with such vague understanding of what it means. I think in my Harvard lectures I said, "Inspiration is a perfectly good word, *if you know what it means.*" The point is: Why do *I* have inspirations and why doesn't a taxi driver on Broadway have inspirations, too? It's not because God gives me special privileges. It's because I have music going on in my mind all the time.

In Harmonic Practice *you say that in the twentieth century there has been no formulation of a complete theoretical approach to the music; consequently, each piece should be evaluated in its own terms.*

Of course. That's true. In fact, I talked about that with Schoenberg once. We were talking about the twelve-tone system and various questions of that sort, and I had been saying that these principles hadn't been formulated. I said, "It will be at least another twenty-five years before they are." He said, "I would say fifty or a hundred years."

This conversation probably took place in 1948 or 1949, because I didn't see Schoenberg again after '49. I don't know whether this was the last time I talked to him or not. So the twenty-five years have passed. But, of course, the difficulty that I find today is this: When people talk about musical theory and refer to the past, they are really referring to working principles that composers used and wrote books about like Johann Jacob Fux's. But he was primarily a composer—well, a lot of analysts are not composers at all. Some of them think they are, but aren't really. [laughter] If you know what I mean.

Are you wary of analysis written by musicologists?

Yes. Well, I mean, analysis is fine so long as it comes as a matter of very close, careful observation of what actually goes on in a piece of music, but when people begin forming rules and so forth, principles, then look out, that's all I'd say. The greatest virtue that an analyst can possess is discretion. The main thing to remember is that that is not the way music is made. It's an analysis of the result, but the process is *entirely* a different one. The first duty of an analyst is to really understand the music, and they don't always. They don't always even bother to absorb the music before they analyze it, or to know it well. And of course, that's where the danger comes in. After you know a piece of music and have taken it in in the normal way, which is listening to it and getting attached to it and enjoying it in one way or another—that's a very, very indefinite word, but I mean getting something out of it, let's say—then you're equipped to analyze it.

Your music is especially difficult to analyze because it does not lend itself to one definable approach.

No, one's got to take it on its own terms, but on terms that always stem from the musical impact of the piece. And not deal with the so-called elements of music, as if they were separate things. That's the trouble with much theorizing nowadays. I mean that you consider harmony, melody, rhythm; they're *not* things that exist in themselves.

Are you, by any chance, referring to a book that does this by your former student, Jan LaRue, called Guidelines for Style Analysis?²

No; I don't want to. These things aren't separate at all, any more than hydrogen and oxygen are separate elements in water. You can't deal with water, one's experience of water for any purpose whatever, by talking about hydrogen and oxygen. You can take the water and make hydrogen and make oxygen from it. Be careful not to light a match, of course! And when it comes to dynamics, that's not a separate thing at all. Rhythm is not a separate thing; none of these things are.

I'd say, first of all, one's got to think of music, in a way, as gesture. Naturally, it's a gesture regulated in such a way that makes sense.

You mentioned that you may have been the first person to introduce Schenker's concepts into this country. What exactly did you mean by that?

I mean that I used it in teaching when very few people had even heard of Schenker here. It may be that he had some disciple over at the Mannes School; there was a man there who was very much a disciple. Teachers didn't use it generally. If Schenker was mentioned, it was in courses in his theory, perhaps, although I must say that musicology wasn't very developed in the United States at that time—maybe it was just beginning to be. I think people were beginning to learn about it. Furthermore, that's not musicology; it's theory. It's very advanced theory, of course. As far as I know, I was the first composer to teach it to composition pupils. I'm quite sure of that, because there were very few composers at that time still, and they were going along very different lines. I was quite alone in my attitude and my point of view. Most of them had studied with Nadia Boulanger, who was the farthest possible from Schenker. She emphasized quite different things. I wouldn't dream of announcing that I was the first one, but I was the first one that I ever heard of.

Of course, I always had my reservations about Schenker. Then they got stronger and stronger as time went on. Schenker is based on the notion that there was really no music before Bach, that everything was primitive before Bach—very, very near-sighted. And that everything was completely gone when Brahms died. It's based on those premises really, and one shouldn't ever forget it.

> *Although attempts have been made to apply it to music past Brahms.*

That is far-fetched, I think. If you have been aware of the elements in music that Schenker was talking about, certainly you're influenced by them, I'm very sure. In my music it is simply an awareness of line. It's not knowledge in the usual sense of the word; it's awareness. Of course, that's what a composer's got to have. He can have the knowledge, too, but if the knowledge is a substitute for awareness, then it's no use to him. Schenker was one of these Germans who thought that, in order to justify a theory, you've got to prove the whole universe by it. I don't think that's true at all.

> *I don't know that many theories would prove the whole universe.*

You don't have to go to the profoundest depths of philosophy in order to justify a thing like that; it's the results that justify it. Also, I think Schenker forces his theory at certain points. The minute these things become dogmatic, then they're in great danger. Because one little exception will wreck the whole business. If you're going to try to justify it on intellectual or philosophical terms, then you're on slippery ground. Naturally, I'm overstating this a little bit.

What he does is to make a big contribution to the

knowledge of how we hear music. If you want to say to the knowledge of the elements that help music to make sense, that's the same thing. I think to stick to the world of human experience is more sound than to try to go into cosmic theory.

He lays much too much stress on the acoustic properties of sounds. It's not the acoustic properties of sounds that are important, it's the human experience in hearing sounds and dealing with them that's important. Schoenberg fell into the same trap when he justified his more complicated harmonies in terms of the upper notes of the overtone series. I can't see any real connection there; I think it's the evolution of musical practice both in composing and in listening that leads to all of this. It's something historical, not something physical or philosophical.

You see why I think every intellectual worker should empty out all his files every ten years or so and reshuffle them and get a new set of folders and arrange them differently. You see what I mean?

Yes. But I wonder if such constant reshuffling would tend to produce chaos among knowledge that's already been established.

Well, of course. You've got to keep creating new worlds.

Diminished seventh cords and augmented sixth chords are both ambiguous. A diminished seventh can be in any of four keys, and it can be even more than that if you go to a secondary harmony in one of these keys. Then there is the so-called German sixth, the augmented sixth chord. Years ago, in one of my classes at Princeton, we invented the "Austrian sixth": The Austrian sixth was the same as the German sixth as far as the sound was concerned. With the German sixth you had F, A, C, D♯, but if you had F, A, B♯, D♯, that made the resolution an A major chord instead of an A minor chord. Then it was an Austrian sixth, because Vienna is a much gayer place than Berlin. [laughter]

I have the metronome with me today because we're going to discuss tempi in my *Falstaff* course.

Tempo markings are always a big problem, especially with Beethoven.

I think there's a very easy explanation of that. The metronome was invented when Beethoven was in mid-career. It was something quite new and he used it. I think his tempi are apt to be too fast. That's the problem. It was the last movement of my second sonata that taught me how to use the metronome. You read music very fast, in about a third of the time that it takes to play it or to hear it. You read it and you aren't expending a tenth of the energy you're expending when you're listening. The physical impacts of the sounds—they've got to begin and end. When you look at the music, that's not there.

When did you first learn about the twelve-tone system?

I suppose I first heard about it in the early twenties, about the time I was writing *The Black Maskers,* or just before. I used to read much more than I do now. There was a French magazine called *La Revue Musicale;* it was very good. They spoke of it.

And furthermore, I *did* know the works of Schoenberg slightly, but I just felt that I wasn't ready to cope with it at all. Then in 1928 I heard a concert after which the two pieces that stayed in my memory were a piece of Schoenberg and one of Stravinsky. The Schoenberg was the minuet from the suite, which is still not at all a favorite piece of mine. The Stravinsky piece was his piano sonata, which I think is a big bore. After the concert it was those pieces that stuck in my mind, and I tried to figure out why they did, because I thought the Schoenberg was alien. It wasn't *so* alien, because I was definitely getting away from Stravinsky in a way.

I never was influenced by Schoenberg in that way; I just got to know that music, that's all. I pinched myself and said, "You're a young composer still, and there's a whole part of the musical world that you don't really know much about." So I got all Schoenberg's piano pieces and I learned opp. 23, 25, 19, and 11 by heart. When I got to Berlin afterwards [in 1931], I found a lot of people who expressed themselves very, very strongly for Schoenberg, but I found I knew these pieces better than they did.

Schoenberg is one of the very great composers, because he's a composer who always gives you something new when you go back to it. I can't feel that way about Stravinsky at all. I can go back with pleasure to Stravinsky, but I don't ever find there are new discoveries in it. He was a great composer, too, undoubtedly, but . . .

There is no twelve-tone idiom; every composer has his own idiom. But of course, all these words are so confused, they're so loosely used. The word "style" is hopelessly confused. This business of style analysis: If it is style, it can't be analyzed. What they call "style analysis" is vocabulary. Vocabulary is a very broad term, too.

> *In Edward T. Cone's article in* Tempo[3] *on your concertino, he writes about dissonance within the twelve-tone system. In other words, notes out of order with the series are resolved* into *a note that comes in the series, an idea of resolution that I thought was very interesting.*

Of course, the series is a point of departure for me always. It's certainly organized, but very freely organized, because I don't ever let myself be bamboozled by it. I mean, I wouldn't change anything that I wanted to write just so as to bring it in line with the series at that point. The main object of the series is that all the notes are always there in the offing, very closely in the offing, and also that they're there where they have to be. And it would be worse if they weren't there, you see. That's one way in which one achieves tension. But I mean the series is always there. It can be found, generally, with a little work.

> *If that's the case, then this notion of twelve-tone resolution wouldn't really be very applicable to* your *music. It would be more applicable to music that was very strictly twelve-tone.*

Well, I think that's a matter of semantics, really. [Cone] is a very intelligent and a very thoughtful man. I don't analyze my own music because it would be such a bore to do it, mainly. And furthermore, I'm not interested in it. I think that this is roughly like Schoenberg's idea. For instance, in his string trio, which I've studied a lot and studied with students a lot, it took me a long time before I was quite sure exactly what the row was. It's there. Once you know it, why, you find it very easily. But the row is one's own possession, one is not possessed by the row. [laughter] Except to the extent that one carries it around with one all the time.

Dallapiccola told me once of a student of his at Queens College. (Every now and then we would meet in New York for a drink.) One day he told me he had met one of his students that morning, and the student told him, "Oh, Maestro, I've started using the row." And Dallapiccola said, "Oh, that's very interesting. What's the row?" This boy fumbled in all his pockets here and there, and finally he said to Dallapiccola, "Well, I haven't got it with me now." And Dallapiccola thought that was awfully funny. And it is, although that's the way some people interpret the row, you see.

When you carry it around with you, do you think of it in terms of the specific pitches of what's known as the prime or original form, or do you think of it as the succession of intervals?

I think of it as a succession of intervals, naturally. Certainly, the row has an original form, and you get it by creative methods, so to speak, to use a word I dislike very much. You get it because of an original musical idea. Then you work on that idea. If it's not quite right, you find out what is right, and that makes the row. Eliminate awkward intervals both in the large and the small. If you don't like the first note, its relation to the fourth note, because of the notes that come in between, you find out something that *does* work. It's a process that Beethoven used certainly, and Bach used in a different way, because we know something about their sketches, not in relation to a twelve-tone row at all.

Then you find out what you want. You have harmonies, and if the notes in the harmonies include certain notes in the row, then you make the harmony so you get the effect you want. If you have to borrow a note that comes in later on, you borrow that. And there are little adjustments, and the row evolves that way. It's always a little different. And then one carries it around in one's head all the time.

> *At the original pitch level? After you've gotten the musical idea and reduced it to the row form, does it stay in your head as the various pitches of the row?*

Well, I would say as little as possible. I mean, I would carry the inversion in my head and octave transpositions as freely as possible. You get so that you have as many resources as you want.

> *Does the row affect the form of your music?*

It does influence the form of a piece, and it can be used that way. The whole province of aural organization is somewhat independent of serialism. The point is that, whatever shape the series takes in a given situation, it doesn't mean that any one basic relationship or any two or three basic relationships are inevitably predominant. There is a general shape, and this gives a set of relationships, but it doesn't establish sharp contrasts the way tonality does. What tonality means to me is that it gives a very definite, sharp framework for the organization of contrasts. I think it's other elements, more than the row itself, that play—this is a very subtle and delicate point—at least an equal role in organizing contrasts.

What do you think of total serialism?

The organization of a piece of music is in the music itself. Dynamics are devices that show you how to illuminate the shape of a piece and to model the phrases. They aren't something that you can treat as a separate entity. That's my fundamental objection to total serialism, because music is a unity, it's a chemical combination. It's not a recipe containing spices, and vegetables, and sauces, and whole lots of different things. It's a chemical combination.

The whole notion of total serialism, that's sheer nonsense. Because in the first place, you can't serialize things that are part of the movement of the piece. It doesn't mean that no good music can be written doing that, but if people want to tie themselves up hand and foot and still produce good music, all right. But it can't be done very much. It's a tour de force.

Theoretically the prime form of the row is as equal as any of the other forty-seven transpositions and permutations of the row. But musically it doesn't usually work out that way. Usually, the prime form, because it gets stated first, or sometimes the piece ends with the retrograde of the prime form . . .

Not necessarily, but that's a very logical way to end. Very often I do. I wouldn't say whether I always do, I don't know.

> *Musically it works out that the prime form* does *have more importance as a succession of pitches than the other transpositions and inversions do.*

Yes. For instance in *Montezuma,* as I was going on I discovered that I had four trichords right there in the first measure. [See the example on page 141.] I wasn't tremendously aware that I had four groups with three notes there. Now, taking the trichords, let's arrange them in a certain order. The first trichord contains two semitones, chromatic. The second trichord has one semitone and a whole tone. The third trichord has one semitone and a major third, in other words, four semitones of a major third and the other a major second. The last one has two major seconds. OK. The minute I became aware of it I found I could shuffle these trichords around. In its original form the row isn't a symmetrical [combinatorial] row. But if I use the first and third together and the second and fourth together, that makes one symmetrical row. If I use one and four together and two and three together, that makes *another* symmetrical row. And of course, that gives you a lot to work with. And then I felt that this was the first area of freedom I have. The second area would be to use the hexachords separately, shuffle them up together. And then the final is to shuffle all the twelve notes up together. Very frequently the original form is there, it comes back. And also, you work on one part of the row, that's another area of freedom. And you keep that in place and use the other notes very freely.

That's the way *Montezuma* ends, as a matter of fact. It ends on the third of those trichords and the first one is down in the bass.

For instance, in the *Divine Comedy* Dante has what he called the *terza rima.* I'd have to think a little while to describe it to you. But he has stanzas of three lines, and then each line rhymes twice with following lines. But it isn't three plus three plus three for one voice; it's three plus three plus three; another voice, it's two plus three plus three plus three; another voice, it's one plus three plus three plus three. So it makes a very intricate pattern. Now, it's a very great poem. Nobody ever has questioned that scheme. The twelve-tone system is more like something like that than anything else. It's not mathematical at all, any more than any music is. After all, there are seven white keys and five black keys. And there are all sorts of ways of combining these within a sort of basic twelve-tone scheme.

> *Let's take for example measure 51 in the second quartet. Three of its lines are accountable to either of the two "rows." But it's free counterpoint. What types of criteria did you use to determine its vertical relationships?*

I think *movement,* which nobody ever speaks about. Movement means movement in every sense of the word. Perhaps nobody speaks about it because it's such a complicated thing. It's something that one has to think of in terms of everything: dynamics, accents, everything. The movement is the final aspect which gives the music its character mostly. *If* there weren't a crescendo here in measure 51 in the cello, you wouldn't have the accents in the first violin.

There's a German word, *Steigerung,* that means accumulation. It includes crescendo and accelerando; it means intensification, really. It doesn't mean necessarily all these things at the same time. What I fight against a little is the habit of thinking of all these so-called elements, or as the word went, "parameters," at one time, as separate things. They aren't at all; they are all inseparable elements of a whole. If you're going to understand the music, you can't think of them separately.

I thought about this a lot in the 1950s. I have some friends in Princeton who are mathematicians and very much involved in the mathematical world. One of our very best friends is the widow of an old friend of mine. She edits the *Mathematical Review,* and her house is always full of mathematicians, sometimes very distinguished ones, because Princeton has a lot of them around. One day I met a very nice man, who's a very distinguished mathematician, and our friend Natasha Brunswick was there, too, and so I said, "Look, I've got you two together now. Please tell me what a parameter is." And they told me. And I said, "All right, Natasha, next time I see you I'm going to tell *you* what a parameter is, and you tell me whether it's right or not." So I said, "Does it have anything to do with dynamics and accents and pitches in music?" They said, "No, not anything whatever."

Another example is what happened when I was in Berlin with the performance of *Montezuma.* It ends with a chorus of clouds, in which the voices are supposed to float. They decided the safest thing to do was to put it on tape. And the tape was finally brought into one of the last rehearsals, and the conductor turned around to me afterwards and said, "Sessions. The tape sounds terrible! *Es klingt schrecklich!*" I said, "I agree with you perfectly. It sounds awful." So what to do about it? The problem was rather nicely solved. Unfortunately, it being in Germany, the tape didn't float. It went [here he sings heavy thumps]. That was the only thing, but it was fairly good.

Anyway, they sent the acoustician of the opera house up to my seat, and I said, "One thing the tape needs is more contrast." He said, "Oh, you can't have more contrast. The tape is difficult enough to listen to, anyway. The ear can take in just so much information." I said, "Look, contrast is not information at all. It's inflection." We fixed it up all right, but this seemed to be the strangest idea I'd ever heard. If you mark *piano* when you hear a crescendo, a listener, if he's really listening to music, doesn't say to himself, "Oh, this is crescendo now." He hears the music getting louder, that's all. It's not information in any sense of the word.

> *Do you first hear polyrhythms that you then figure out a way of notating, or do you arrive at a texture through some other means?*

I try to write it the way I hear it.

> *Well, do you hear each of the polyrhythmic lines discretely or in combination?*

Both, I would say. That's the only way I can put it.

I had a very good discussion once with Eduard Steuermann. We had a friend who was a very gifted conductor and who, I'd been told, would take a complicated rhythmic passage—for instance, two voices that go together (that occurs quite often in my music where they're rhythmically different)—and he would work them out mathematically. I said to Eduard, "That is not what I want. If I write a very slow triplet over a certain passage, what I want is a certain gesture. I don't want the notes to be mathematically, absolutely on the dot." I was thinking of a passage in the *Idyll of Theocritus;* it was just after I'd written that. [sings the three notes] Steuermann laughed and said, "You remind me of something that happened when I was playing Berg's double concerto once." (Actually, I heard that performance in Berlin, with him and Kolisch.) He had a passage where he had to play three rhythms at once. He said, "I just couldn't work it out myself, so I went to Berg and I said, 'Look, you've got to help me with this. I can't do it by myself.' Berg said, 'Oh, but that's not what I want. I just don't want them to be together.'" And that's it.

If you play a lot of what are called dissonant intervals and suddenly hit an octave, it functions almost in the way that a dissonance used to function in tonal music.

But you don't hear that in my music.

In your music there are frequently irregular groupings of the beat and polyrhythms, and when one gets suddenly to a place in which it's regular . . .

It's like eating ice cream the way we used to make it when I was a child. You would twist it around a bucket of ice with a lot of salt in the ice. Every now and then you'd taste a piece of ice with some salt in it. It's like that. [laughter] It sounds fortuitous, doesn't it, unless it's very, very carefully intended by a composer? I suppose you can do that on purpose, conceivably. You can have a triad appear and not disturb the texture, unless it comes on a very prominent accentuated place; then it could disturb it. One of the morals of that is: Correct the proofs very carefully.

Your first piano sonata contains three-voice writing. Would you say in general that three-voice counterpoint is a medium which you favor?

No, not necessarily three voices. It's a little hard to say this in very accurate terms. But I think that the ear *really* grasps three different things at a time. Now, those aren't necessarily voices. I find the legend that good counterpoint is counterpoint in which all the voices are equally important untrue. That may be theoretically all right, but it doesn't turn out that way in practice.

Manfred Bukofzer was my great antagonist in the California music department. I had some students who distinguished themselves, and he was, if I may say so, a very jealous man. We used to have arguments, and he used to bait me—he was always needling me. One night we were talking about counterpoint. I said, "The idea of the equality of the voices in Renaissance counterpoint is a legend. It's not really true, because in the first place the outer voices have to be predominant." And he said, "That's where you composers always make that mistake. This has been true for the last four hundred years, but it was never true before then." And I said, "But of course it was *always* true." It got to the point where he was saying it wasn't and I was saying it was. So finally I said,

"Tell me, if that's true, why was the six-four chord never considered the equivalent of a triad?" He said, "Oh, you're talking about the ear. The ear has no importance in these matters." Now I'm sure he was being a little incautious, because he had gotten excited. We used to have arguments like that. And arguments about terminology. He was the kind of German who thought he knew more about the English language than anybody else. We used to have arguments about *that,* too.

You said that the ear can hear, of course, three parts. Do you draw a limit? Do you think it cannot hear any more, for instance, than four or five parts?

You *hear* everything, but there are three voices, which as voices take precedence, that's all.

Beyond three voices, you feel that there's more of a flow?

Yes. It's more of a general flow, I would say. This is not a *rule,* but I think it's a *fact.* It wouldn't inhibit me in anything I chose to write. There are only two different directions in which voices can move, or three. They can stand still, or move up, or move down. Perhaps that is what it really amounts to. But the voices are generally organized in such a way that there are no more than three sorts of major happenings at a time. You see what I mean. Now, within each of these three there can be irregularities in movements. I don't think analysts discover the truth. They discover, oh, directions.

In my music I achieve flexibility after I've established the tempo. Polyrhythmic is really polyphonic. There is an example in the *Eroica* Symphony. The one beat that doesn't need to be accentuated is the first beat of a measure. I would consider that common sense, because there's a lot of common nonsense. (I won't say uncommon sense.) [laughter] Ritenuto means hold back; rallentando means gradually get slower. These things are not totally precise, but you can't be totally precise. Fortissimo doesn't always mean the same thing. It certainly doesn't mean the same thing on every instrument. I think *Montezuma* was the first piece in which I put the glossary of musical indications, because there were so many things wrong with the Berlin performance.

You can't have more than three separate elements in the foreground. In my music I'd say there are not more than perhaps two important things in the foreground. The rest is modification. Say you have a noun and a verb and the rest are adjectives.

How would you define the often-used phrase "to know a piece of music"?

I would say that to know it "by heart" is to know the music. For example, I know Debussy's *Pelléas and Mélisande* and Beethoven's C-sharp minor quartet by heart.

I've just been teaching the C-sharp minor quartet in my course here at Juilliard. I pointed out that in the early classical music the concept of the relative minor places the emphasis in the wrong direction. C major and C minor are essentially almost identical; they're the same key in different coloring, because C is always the tonic. But C major and A minor are different keys. And it's the relation of the third—the scale happens to be the same, but the relationships within the scale are not. Beethoven is extraordinarily free with this because very often passages occur where, if one is very precise about it, the tonal region is one in which C-sharp minor and E major flow back and forth. Here on the first page of the score, Beethoven made an apparent cadence in E major, but he leads it right back to C-sharp minor here. All this is apparently in E major. At the end of the second movement of the Eighth Symphony, there's a long excursion into the subdominant harmony. The tonic comes back at the end so suddenly that, before one knows the piece very well, one feels that it ends on the dominant. I remember always thinking, "That really ends in the dominant of E-flat." And then suddenly one day I realized that I knew the piece well enough and remembered the B-flat major beforehand. It came out absolutely right in the tonic from then on for me. So already with Beethoven the tonal concept was beginning to dissolve.

Like ultimately everything else analysis is highly subjective. Because we're human beings and we have eyes, and that's what we see with, but they're part of our bodies. And our minds, too. All this is highly subjective, that's all. If people recognize that, that's the main thing. There's no such thing as a really objective approach to any of the arts. Even science is extremely subjective. Because it's human beings who are faced with objects, and if the objects are very important to you, it becomes subjective in that sense. It's the human beings who make these judgments. It's somewhat frightening in some of its aspects. That's the world we live in, that's all.

I wrote several letters to the Journal of the American Musicological Society *trying to get my article on* The Black Maskers *published. The editor stressed that the article shouldn't have very much subjective analysis in it. I wrote back saying, "The only thing that I said subjectively was that I thought a certain part sounded like Debussy, but the rest of it is fairly straightforward."*

Everything is subjective connected with the music. This distinction between subjective and objective is really a lot of nonsense when it comes to the arts. Even in science no human being can make a judgment or anything without having his own personality come into it. This works reasonably well up to a certain point, but it's really nonsense; it has no logic or reason behind it at all. You see what I mean?

Oh yes. There's even a theory about psychologists who administer tests in which their own predispositions affect the results.

I saw in the *Times* an op-ed page article about Lincoln by a psychologist from Texas who's analyzing Lincoln's hidden motives in seeking the presidency, completely from an un-reconstructed southerner's point of view. It was ridiculous; it made Lincoln out to be not exactly a scoundrel, but a cheap little egocentric who was venting his frustrations on the American nation. Well, that is utterly nonsense. Everybody knows that in any decision he made . . . I mean one's motives are highly complex. But you can have very good ones. Furthermore, it wasn't Lincoln who forced the South to secede from the Union; they did it of their own accord.

Of course, there's been an awful lot of sentimentality about the old South. They had nice magnolia trees and beautiful Spanish moss and some very nice people, but it was really based on brutality. It was the same way in other parts of the world. The North was not guiltless of a lot of things, especially after the Civil War. Lincoln was a very, very great man and he was also a man who was not corrupted by power—about the only big political figure who wasn't. I don't think Roosevelt was. You know the very wise statement by Lord Acton. "Power corrupts, and absolute power corrupts absolutely." That's absolutely true. Look at the shah, after all.

6

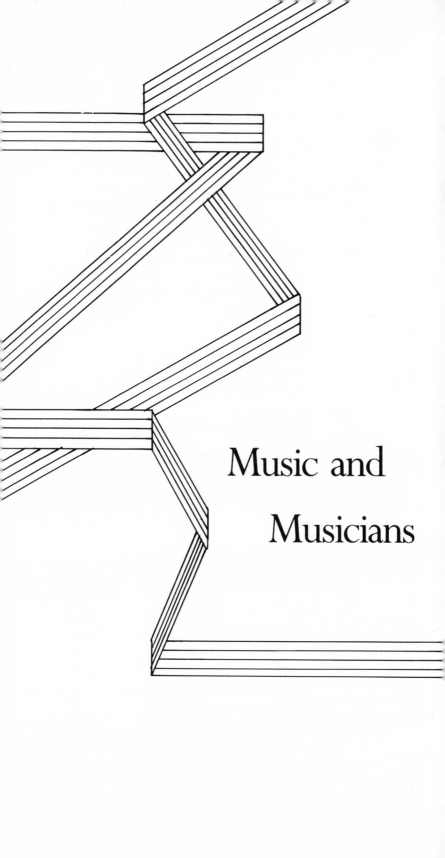

Music and

Musicians

Do you think there is an American quality to your work?

I never worried about that. Now, Aaron Copland said that I didn't worry about it because I come from an old family, and that is *undoubtedly* part of my life, because I realized that with that background I always had a basic sense of social security—security in American society. And it's too late to become uneasy about American society, although there are plenty of reasons to feel upset by it today. I've had American tradition from the day I was born. Everything that we had was local, and if it were other than local, it was *national.* I was always fascinated by the Civil War—a supreme instance of human folly at its most widespread.

Anything I did and put my whole self into must have something American about it. I didn't go to Europe until I was twenty-seven years old. I studied here in this country with a European.

What is really national, if you want to call it that, is the character that gradually develops in a national idiom. And I've never worried about being either nationalistic or individual, because I think I am. I know damn well I am, if I may say so. I don't believe in being self-conscious about these things, because if you're self-conscious about them, then the music becomes essentially contrived.

I would like to discuss further this concept of being an American composer. What does that mean, an American composer? How do you define Americanism musically?

There was a time when people said I wasn't really American because I was here before the Revolution, so to speak, which is really nonsense. I do have these memories in my family. My grandmother's great grandfather was a general in the Revolution. I'm sorry to say he lost the battle of Charleston, South Carolina, but he couldn't help it. His name was Benjamin Lincoln; he was the first secretary of war, but not under the presidency, under the Confederation before the Constitution was written.

The point is—maybe this is the most important thing—that a composer should develop naturally and without any forced adoption of either technique or style. I was glad I came to the twelve-tone technique by degrees and used it for my own purposes. I never tried to force myself into a style, or anything like that, because I wanted to find my own style. And I believe in that very, very much. If you get self-conscious about these things, it's not a good idea; then the music tends to come from a much less profound level in the personality.

Of course, that's the way it always was in the past until the middle of the nineteenth century, which was when, out of very, very genuine impulses, people began being interested in the folk music of their own countries. But we have to face the fact that we *don't* really have any folk music in this country. What we call folk music here is on a much more sophisticated level; these aren't songs that have been sung by people for a thousand years. They're nice songs, sometimes, which have become popular. I mean, Stephen Foster lived a little over a hundred years ago and his songs became very popular. These are sung. And the Negro spirituals are the nearest, I would say, that we have. But they were in a way adaptations of Protestant hymn tunes. We can't really talk about American folk music. I think the influence of folk music on European music has been vastly exaggerated sometimes.

I think there are certain things that we have absolutely naturally. One of my ideas is that national character in music derives primarily from the language and the rhythm of the language spoken. That's why even in Italian opera you have phrases that more often than not end on the weak beat of the measure, because for the most part a very large majority of Italian words are accented on the next to the last syllable. Very few are accented on the last syllable. There's always an accent on the letter when that happens, as in *città* and *virtù*.

> *But you believe that this carries over into instrumental music, too?*

Of course. This is just the shape that it comes in. Probably there is a tendency toward certain rhythmic things. Certainly in my own music there's a lot of syncopation. But I don't force myself to prefer a syncopated line to an unsyncopated one, that's all.

That's my feeling about the whole thing. The whole history of culture is that it develops in certain centers, and then other centers take it over—it becomes a little different. Musical history developed very much in the late Middle Ages up along the North Sea and on both sides of the English Channel. Then in the late fifteenth century good people were all offered jobs in Rome, because of the Vatican. Then Italian music began developing: madrigals, and of course church music, and Orlando di Lasso. So the center passed gradually to Italy. Then of course somewhat later the Germans developed. But still, in the eighteenth century Handel and Mozart went to study in Italy. Bach studied the music of Vivaldi (God knows why).

> *Where does music flourish in the twentieth century?*

That's difficult. Of course, the Viennese school still went on, and the French at a certain time seemed to develop very much, especially after the Franco-Prussian War. On the other hand, I don't think France ever produced a greater composer than Berlioz. Of course, earlier there was Couperin and Rameau, Gluck and Lully (who came from Florence but he lived in Paris around Louis XIV). People weren't so fussy about nationalism, but national character just developed; I think that's the way it should be.

But very often our most gifted writers were appreciated in Europe before they were appreciated in this country. Up to a certain point that's still true. I probably told you about when I was fourteen, just about to enter Harvard, I met this very wealthy lady from Chicago, whose sister-in-law married Theodore Thomas, the founder of the Chicago Orchestra, and she thought she knew everything. She didn't know very much really, but she begged me from the bottom of her heart to give up all ideas of being a composer, because an American couldn't be a composer, you see. When I told my European friends that story, they always whooped with laughter, because of course it's nonsense.

Especially after the First World War my own story was somewhat different, because I would have gone to study in Europe if the First World War hadn't broken out. But I didn't, I couldn't, obviously, under the circumstances. I finally studied with Ernest Bloch, who was the most distinguished European composer living in this country. I'm glad I did, because if I at the age of eighteen had gone to France to study, considering how little I knew anyway and the kind of training I'd had, I don't know what would have happened. I think I would have been swamped, sort of. And I *still* don't think France was the best place to go to study.

*So many American composers went to study with Nadia
Boulanger.*

I never thought that she was anything less than a quite
remarkable musician, except that she was not excep-
tional in that respect in Europe. She was the first European who really took seriously American students. If I
may say so, somewhat cynically, she made a very good
thing out of it.

I never considered Nadia Boulanger as really a teacher
of mine. She wasn't. At one time I thought I'd like to
study with her, and she refused and said, "You're Bloch's
pupil." I was always a friend. I went there; she seemed
very friendly. However, what happened started this way:
The ISCM [International Society for Contemporary Mu-
sic] was a much more important thing at that time than
it is now. It was really started after the First World War
with musicians from various countries, one of whom
was a very good friend of mine and introduced me to
Schnabel and to Klemperer and to Monteux, and so
forth. But he and a lot of people thought that this society
would bring the composers of Europe back into contact
with each other again. Then later a United States section
was formed, which is another story, because I had a very
funny relationship with the United States section at first.

Now, in 1933, the year before I left Berlin, the ISCM
festival was to be in Amsterdam. The festival the year
before was in Vienna. And naturally there was a meeting
after the Vienna festival, and the jury was to be chosen
for the following year. My First Symphony was submitted by Ansermet independently, who was a member of
the jury, and chosen. And nothing else the American
section submitted was chosen.

The next year a delegate, Fred Jacobi (who was a

friend of mine; some of the other people from the American section were mad) wanted to put me up for the jury. I said to him, "I'm of two minds about this. I don't really care, but if you want to put me up, go ahead." So he went to the president of the ISCM, Edward Dent. He was enthusiastic about the idea and put my name on the slate. Jacobi told me about this, and I said, "I'm not sure that I want to be on this, because it could be very embarrassing for me to be on the same jury with Nadia Boulanger. Some music by her pupils might be submitted, and I might not agree with her, and I don't want to get into a fight with her."

Jacobi said to Casella, "Don't you think Nadia Boulanger is very, very prejudiced in favor of her pupils?" I was there, and there was nothing I could do about it. In any case, the vote was taken. I had no vote, I just sat with Fred Jacobi. The ballots were supposedly secret, but the French delegate, Henri Prunières, stood behind the woman who was counting the ballots. He absolutely exploded at Fred Jacobi and myself. He said, "You haven't voted for Mlle. Boulanger. She *made* American music! Up to now I voted for Sessions—but of course that's impossible now." Maybe we were tied, maybe I got one more vote than she did. Anyway, he called for another vote. He said that he thought that somebody should be on it who represented *le point de vue esthetique française*. Three people spoke in my favor: Casella, Malipiero, and Ansermet. The vote was taken: I got one more vote than before and she got two votes less. And I regretted that, because she was a friend of mine.

Shortly after this I went to see her in Paris. I was living in Berlin, and I met her on the outskirts of Paris and she drove me back into the center of town. I said I hated that business that had taken place in Vienna. She said she knew all about it, she didn't want any explanations from me or anything. She gave me what the French call a *mauvais quart d'heure,* a bad quarter of an hour. The *mauvais quart d'heure* lasted exactly a quarter of an hour. We parted on cordial, if not friendly, terms. She invited me to dinner at her place out in the country. I went out there, and she gave me a royal dinner and kissed me on both cheeks when I left. I thought, "Thank God, that's all over."

I went back to Berlin. Two days before it came time to go to Amsterdam for the meeting, I got a letter in a familiar handwriting. It said, "Dear Roger, I count on you for the following." And she had a list of all the works submitted by her students there. I kept that letter. It's in a file I have called "Curiosities."

But then, I actually did vote for one of her students, because I thought he deserved it. Also I voted for something that Dallapiccola had submitted. But it wasn't chosen.

Then came my divorce. The night before I went to court in Reno, Nevada, I had a long letter from her begging me not to. She knew nothing at all about the circumstances. She begged me not to do it, telling me how I'd feel and so forth. I immediately sent that letter to [my wife] Barbara and said, "You take care of that. I think that's for you." Because she was for the divorce, too.

I'm compiling a list of incomplete works of yours. In the mid-twenties you were working on The Fall of the House of Usher.

I was much more attracted by one of the Boccaccio stories from the *Decameron* at that time, and I even made some sketches. But I didn't think of making an opera out of it, as I had been thinking of *The Fall of the House of Usher*. The Boccaccio's a lovely little story about a girl and a young man, and they fall very much in love. They can't get together. She says, "Well, perhaps I can arrange to make a bed out on the porch outside my father's door and sleep there. If I can do that, I can let you know."

So she begins complaining about the heat—it's in May. Her mother tells her, "You don't need to worry about the heat. We get used to that. It's just because it's come on rather suddenly this year. You'll be all right." She sleeps with her mother; so when she goes to bed with her mother she keeps herself awake and is very restless because it's so hot. So the mother tells the father, and the father says, "We'll let her make her bed out on the porch and put a curtain up so that nobody can see in. And I'll lock my door."

So they make a bed with a curtain around it, and she makes a sign to this young man. He scrambles up. It's really quite difficult, but he gets there all right, and they have a very good time all night. Toward morning they fall asleep. (I won't tell you all the details because there's one very amusing little item that is—well, if you're born in 1896, you don't tell these things to ladies.)

Then in the morning they oversleep because they're tired. And the parents get impatient because she hasn't appeared, and the father says, "Well, I'll go out there and see if she's all right." He goes out there, and they're there lying in bed together in a state of great intimacy. The father says nothing; he's shocked a little. He goes back to the mother and says, "Now you come with me, but promise me you won't say a word, you won't make any noise." He goes out and wakes them up, and they're absolutely horrified because the young man thinks he might be put to death for this. The father tells the mother, "This is a nice young man and he's got plenty of money, and she'll be very happy with him." They've wondered whom she should marry. So he says, "You let me take care of it; it will be all right."

The father upbraids them and says, "There's only one way you can make up for this, unless you want to lose your life, and that's if you marry each other on the spot." He takes a ring off his finger and gives it to this young man, and he puts it on the finger. I guess in those days— this was the fourteenth century, of course—that you could have a ceremony before the church ceremony. So he marries them on the spot. He says, "Now go back to bed together and have a good time." [laughter]

It's a very nice story, and I was enchanted by it, but I didn't know how it could be set to music. Some details obviously would have to be omitted. Nevertheless, it's a lovely story, a well-known story. The point is, she wants to listen to the nightingale, and the father says, "Why shouldn't she? She's a young girl and would enjoy listening to the nightingale, and it would help her to sleep." There's a little joking about the nightingale involved, too.

The whole setting of the *Decameron* involves the plague, which is going on furiously in Florence, and these ten young people—I think three men and seven young women—decide they are going to go and occupy a villa, which is at their disposal. The villa's been identified; it's called the Villa Palmieri. I guess they're all pretty well off. They have servants and they keep separate quarters, they live in virtue, according to the story, although they all know about life. I guess in those days, especially in Italy, people were much more frank about things than they have been at certain periods, notably in the nineteenth century in Europe.

Each day one of them is appointed the king or the

queen of the day. Then each one of them tells a story on a certain subject chosen by the king of the day. This story is told by a young man named Filostrato and the queen of the day is a very lively young woman named Ninfale. I think the subject that day was to tell stories about young lovers who go through bad adventures but finally everything comes out all right.

I think those are the most wonderful stories in the world, and I think they're the most beautifully told. This is a classic. It wasn't allowed to be sold in the United States until 1930, and then there was a big protest from everybody, because it's a classic. Chaucer and Shakespeare all borrowed stories from it. *All's Well That Ends Well* is a story from the *Decameron*. These stories influenced literature all over Europe. *Gianni Schicchi* of Puccini is a story from the *Decameron*. They're not all stories about—well I hate the word "sex"—at all. In one of them, even in my edition, the crucial part is kept in the original Italian. It's a very, very funny story— highly pornographic. It makes fun of the clergy too, very much.

Which in the fourteenth century was corrupt. The Roman de Fauvel *does that, too.*

In the introduction there's a wonderful description of what the plague was like in Florence; it was awful. In this book of Barbara Tuchman's,[1] she quotes from the *Decameron*. It's a wonderful book. Sometimes I just take it out and read one of the stories, unless it's one I know too well already.

You were thinking of setting this story to music . . .

225

Making a sort of ballet out of it.

Did you read it in the Italian or in a translation?

I read it in Italian. It's very difficult Italian; it's much more difficult than Dante is. And there are even some disputed passages in the translation, because it's very local, although Boccaccio traveled all over Europe and wrote a lot of other things. He wrote the first big commentary on the *Divine Comedy*. After all, he was born very shortly after Dante died.

Was it while you were living in Italy that this particular story appealed to you as a possible ballet?

I'm not sure. I *think* it was while I was living in Italy.

But you abandoned the notion?

Yes. I think I even made a few sketches, but I had other things in mind. I was going to write that after I got through with my First Symphony.

I recommend the *Decameron*. It's really an enchanting book. In Italy, if there's a slightly piquant little story about illicit love, or something like that—to use another awful phrase—they're apt to call it a *Boccaccescha* story.

Would you comment on your written remarks that "in many respects and from many directions we are developing new conceptions and new criteria—dramatic,

musical, and theatrical—of opera in this century?"[2]
Could you expound upon that idea?

We've been living in very intense political century after all, with two huge cataclysms which completely changed the aspect of the world: the First World War, which began it, and the Second World War, which was really a sort of a denouement of the first. Hitler and the Nazis were never really understood outside of Germany, and not in a way in Germany. Hitler was a demagogue who led a kind of populist movement. The Germans were in very bad shape economically. When I first went to Germany, it was chaos. What a book review I read makes perfectly clear was that Germany was not led by outstanding people, but by very mediocre people. That was the reason why it took the form it did. It was just a demagogue who knew how to appeal to the mob, so to speak, by playing on its worst impulses.

Brecht's text for *The Trial of Lucullus* was really a radio drama which was broadcast over the Zurich radio, I think, while Hitler was invading Poland. I think that fundamentally, in a very profound sense, *Montezuma* and *Lucullus* are about the same subject: the futility of conquest.

There are so many really outstanding operas in the twentieth century, like *Moses and Aron,* like *Wozzeck,* like all three of Dallapiccola's operas. His opera *Il Prigioniero* [*The Prisoner*] has been more widely performed in Europe than any Italian opera since Puccini. It's a political opera; it's an opera about the Inquisition. Dreadful story based on, let's say, inspirations that he had from various things. It's a very powerful story; you don't find anything like that in opera in the nineteenth century.

Fidelio *is in a sense a prison story.*

In a sense, yes. And *Don Carlo* in a sense, of course. But not in the same way, not focusing on that horror. Of course, *Fidelio* has a happy ending. The Dallapiccola opera shows what was on everybody's mind. It was on Borgese's mind in *Montezuma,* too. These operas are quite different from what went before.

You feel that the difference lies mostly in the subject matter?

In the subject matter and the whole tone of the work, and naturally the form and everything else.

Speaking of form, in Montezuma *are there any large-scale forms in the way that there are in* Wozzeck *in which, for example, a symphony in five movements occupies an act?*

That's very, very rough. I could find things like that in *Montezuma* if I wanted to. But it's the kind of text and one's attitude toward the text. That was a very general remark of mine you just quoted, but I thought of works like *Il Prigioniero,* like Dallapiccola's big opera about Ulysses, which has never been performed in this country and it's a very large-scale work. It presents great problems of production, just as *Montezuma* does. I suppose it doesn't represent a general trend, but it represents an attitude on the part of people who've been very much affected by this century. Naturally, *Moses and Aron* is something different, too. But it's about a philosophical question.

You might say they're all a little along the lines of interpreting political events in a broader philosophical scale, if you wanted to put it that way. I don't like any of these terms very much.

> *Reading that, I wondered whether you were thinking of any specific techniques that were being developed in the twentieth century as ways of portraying these events on stage.*

Well, I think that's for other people to find out. One is doing a job at the time. With *Lucullus* I wanted to have the right musical tone and background for each scene as the drama developed. Furthermore, in none of these works, do you have the leitmotiv system. Verdi didn't either, of course. Wagner did. In the weaker moments in Wagner, it becomes a little crude.

The point is that I never felt that I was using a method. With Wagner you *do* feel that he was using a method.

One night I had a very long conversation about opera with a friend of mine, an opera director. We talked for hours about opera—about Mozart and Verdi, and so on. At the end of the evening I suddenly realized, and said to him, "We have been talking of opera all night and have not once mentioned Wagner!"

Opera is a vocal work, Wagner somewhat to the contrary notwithstanding. I listened to part of *Parsifal* on the radio last Sunday, to most of the third act. It didn't come across very well. It's a strange work. I have *awfully* mixed feelings about Wagner.

I have especially mixed feelings about that opera. I had an opportunity two weeks ago to see it again at the Met and I declined.

It is awfully long. I think—if one can ever make such a statement—that it really has the greatest music in it that Wagner ever wrote. There's one wonderful character in it, and that's Kundry. Otherwise it repels me a little; I mean, the whole conception of the characters. It's terribly German in the worst sense of the word.

I agree. That this idiot, this Parsifal, should have anything at all to do with the Holy Grail is annoying.

Of course, that's part of it; he's a "guileless fool." Of course, he isn't entirely an idiot. He goes out and has a little experience in the world. But this whole business about Klingsor, who castrated himself because he couldn't get in otherwise, and of course that disqualified him completely. And Kundry, who is coached by Klingsor to seduce Parsifal. He's a good little boy and doesn't let himself be seduced by her. Naturally, under the circumstances, it was wise but somewhat priggish.

Wagner's poetry is abominable, absolutely dreadful. If I feel in a bad humor, I sometimes think of the line in the *Walküre:* "Wintersturme wichen dem Wonnemond." Germans agree with me about that. He was a *wretched* poet. And he thought he was a poet; he wasn't.

You yourself were something of a pianist.

I have the rudiments of a piano technique, perhaps because of the four-hour session I spent with Schnabel once. It was one of the most interesting experiences I ever had. Schnabel was a dear friend of mine. He knew I was going to give a concert, and he asked me if I would like to play for him before I gave this concert with a cellist. I said, "No, I don't really think I would." He looked sort of crestfallen, and I thought, "What a silly, childish thing that was to say." So the next week I said, "Look, I'm sorry. I behaved like a sixteen-year-old the other day, and I'd love to play for you." He said fine. I asked, "May I bring Mr. Barati, the cellist, and we'll play the Beethoven sonatas?" I was playing some bagatelles, op. 126. I always had lunch with Schnabel in New York on Tuesdays, and I found that he'd made himself free for the whole afternoon. So I called up my students and put them off. And he sat me down at 2:00 and from 2:00 to 6:00 he gave me the works. My cellist said my technique had improved more in those four hours than it had in the four years we'd played together.

He just loosened me up and made me listen to my own playing. I played the Beethoven op. 102 cello sonatas in D major and C major. They're wonderful pieces. The D major started [illustrates by singing]. He said, "Why don't you accent the lower D instead of the high D?" I said, "I thought I did." He said, "Yes, *you* thought you did, but your *thumb* thought otherwise." Then I had a skip in one place in one of the bagatelles. He said, "Don't hurry, just take your time, you'll get down there all right." It was over a bar line, you see. He said, "You don't have to hurry to get down to the low note." Another time I had a passage like this [demonstrates a quiet tremolo passage on the piano]. He said, "Don't move your hand, don't move your hand. It will play itself."

Then in another place, I had to make skips—it was in the slow movement, marvelous slow movement. He

231

said, "But why do you do it that way, why don't you lift up your hand and let it fall on the note?" I said, "I suppose because it would fall in the wrong place." He put his fist on his hips and said, "And what do you think would happen if it fell in the wrong place?!" We had a very good time, and that's as much piano technique as I ever acquired.

Dallapiccola wrote a letter when his opera was performed in Berlin, and he said, "Si sa che la nostra professione è una scuola di pazienza." "One knows that our profession is the school of patience."

Do you think political maneuverings afflict today's musical life in general?

The general society looks upon any serious artistic achievement as essential frivolity.

The great trouble with musical life today is that the orchestras are run, financed, and supported by very wealthy people who are not really very cultivated in any sense generally. Maybe some people are. But they still are living in the nineteenth century, in a certain sense. (All statements like that are suspect.) They still think of art as something very glamorous that comes from somewhere else, some legendary place. And they have been abroad—that's the way people used to talk about going to Europe—and they have come in contact with all this. They may have met a conductor or something, and they think in terms of glamorous personalities, not in terms of music. It's a world that they never really lived in. That, of course, infects the whole of culture in this sense, but especially music. They don't know what a composer is.

And you think that it's these people who fund the orchestras who have some say over the choice of programs?

Yeah. Well, they have to be pleased. I read a statement by a man who was supporting the Philharmonic. Only a few years ago he said: "It should play only the tried and true."

Of course, if it never gets tried, how can one know whether it's true or not?

Yes. But the orchestras are not supposed to waste valuable rehearsal time on music that hasn't been proven to be profitable. Eventually, it all comes down in the end, when you really strip it of all the nonsense, it means what is valuable in terms of . . .

Money.

They ought to know that almost all the really first-class music of the past, even in the eighteenth century, had to make its way gradually. Haydn had a good job, but he didn't really begin to be famous until he was quite old, especially by the standards of that day. Mozart was an infant prodigy, and he became a rather difficult man later on, and he quarreled with his patrons. They make up legends about these things.

I read somewhere the reason Beethoven's quartets weren't appreciated for so long was because quartets weren't any good in those days. Well, look, Beethoven played the violin himself. Of course, when his violinist friend asked him why he wrote for the violin the way he did, Beethoven said, "Do you expect me to think of your damn fiddle when I'm talking to God?" But nobody knows how people played. When you judge by the music written, they must have played pretty damn well. And there's no reason why they shouldn't have. Just because nowadays people negotiate the very high register much more easily than they could then because they have discovered new technical tricks doesn't mean that they didn't play what they could play just as well as anybody can play nowadays. That's the difference.

The more I think about music critics, the more—I won't say exactly my heart goes out to them—but they live an impossible kind of life. You can't go and hear a new piece and immediately write an article; nobody can. I've told you about how I went to see Klemperer one night years ago in Philadelphia. He had to go out for an *hour* in the evening and left me with a pile of scores. On the top of the pile was the *Lulu Suite* of Alban Berg. I opened it and started reading it very carefully. Suddenly Klemperer appeared, and I said, "My God, you've come back, and I've been reading this score all the time. I've only got to page three. How long does it take you to read a score?" He said, "Oh, about that long." [laughter] Naturally, one was reading very carefully and looking at everything that was on the page: the way the score has to be read. This was forty years ago, but I've been reading scores all my life. You can't *possibly* hear a piece for the first time. Sometimes you can.

What was your reaction to Winthrop Sargeant's New Yorker *review of your Eighth Symphony entitled "Is Music Dead?"*[3]

Well, it amused me, because he said I sat on my throne in Princeton and dictated the course of the future of music. I was amused by that because I thought it overstated the case. I mean, he knew more about music than most of the critics around New York, in fact. On older music, I didn't always agree, but he sometimes wrote rather intelligently. You see, people don't understand what goes on, and I don't think they want to understand particularly. They're so enmeshed in, I won't say tradition, but traditionalism, that they just can't understand anything outside that framework at all. They think they know everything, and if there's something they don't understand, they don't grasp with their own ears . . . of course, this is not a phenomenon peculiar to our own time at all.

The study of history proves that.

Of course. Philipp Emanuel Bach thought music was dead. I've forgotten who in Beethoven's time. Alfred Einstein had a friend who thought that music really ended, was hopelessly on the decline, from the middle of Beethoven's career on.

Most teachers don't understand that if you're a composer, you write your own music. You write music that you love, yourself, not music that you think somebody else will approve of. This is terribly important. This is I think very largely an American disease, because I think that's what's the trouble with music in America, with the public, too. In very large part, not universally, of course, but it's simply that music has been something that was imported for too many years. I've told you about that woman who urged me not to be a composer in the teens, because I was an American. Nobody says that nowadays, of course.

> *But you think that perhaps too few composition teachers understand that a student has to write his own music, rather than music that they themselves write?*

Teach them the rules; then tell them, if they're good, that there are no rules or that the rules don't matter. The rules are just pedagogical conveniences at a certain point, that's all. Naturally, you start out learning counterpoint and you start with rules; but you explain that the rules deal with specific problems. If those problems aren't there, you forget about them. Sometimes, if I find that a composer is writing consecutive octaves, or consecutive fifths, and they don't work, I tell him. Not because it's against the rules, but because it's just not good. The rules arose because composers were aware of them, you see. If you really want octaves and write them with a positive intent, then they're almost certain to be good. If you write fifths with a positive intent, they're almost certain to be good. But you have to be aware that they're there, that's all.

> *You were saying that you thought there was a problem in this country teaching composition.*

Some teachers teach them to write *their* music.

I don't know how anybody teaches. I don't know how any of my colleagues teach at all.

> *It's such a personal thing between the personality of the student and the personality of the teacher.*

Absolutely. Of course, there are some students who study with somebody, or at least come to him, because he has a name or something, and they think it will help them in their careers to have studied with so and so. And sometimes they even lie about it a little bit. John Cage advertises himself as a pupil of Schoenberg. Well, he had about two lessons with Schoenberg. Like the Italian story about an organ grinder who was playing in the streets years ago and happened to be right outside the house where Mascagni lived. Mascagni was writing something and didn't want to hear the organ grinder. (Don't misunderstand me: I'm not an admirer of Mascagni at all, but he had a great success for a while.) So he shouted out, "Stop that! I can't stand it!" And so the organ grinder moved on. And then next time he came out, he had a little placard that said, "Pupil of Mascagni." [laughter]

I've listed as a pupil of yours Peter Maxwell Davies. Although you say he's never really formally studied with you, he says he studied with you.

He was in Princeton, and I used to see him quite often. I had a lovely time with him. He's extremely gifted. He's one of the most gifted people living. I told him once, "It's wonderful. I'm delighted to be called a teacher of yours."

It was informal. In a way, my relations with my students are always informal. If I were teaching them harmony or elementary counterpoint, it wouldn't be quite the same way. But I wouldn't be teaching that any more, though.

Nowadays there's too much emphasis on personalities.

237

I wonder sometimes whether people really give a damn about music. That is partly the result of what's known as alienation. One has to have a sense that one is contributing something. In Saul Bellow's acceptance speech for the Nobel Prize, he quoted the Sermon on the Mount, "Woe unto you when all men speak well of you." And so some dissenting voices are reassuring, because if there are no dissenting voices, then that's a sure sign that nobody's gotten very much out of it.

Leonard Bernstein knows that I disagree with him rather fundamentally. And he disagrees with me very fundamentally. He's been pursuing success; I've been pursuing accomplishment. Now that sounds a little pompous, but it's the only way of putting it succinctly. I don't give a hoot about success.

Alexander the Great wished that his people regard him and worship him as a god. The Spartans thought, "If Alexander wants to be regarded as a god, he should act like one." If you want to be something, then you try to be it, instead of being known as it. Don't worry what people think.

Sarah Caldwell told me that she was taken to see the place where Shostakovich lived, and he had a picture of me on his desk. It's awfully nice; I feel very touched. I didn't really know him. When we were over there in Moscow, we were not allowed to see him, so to speak, until the very last day and when there was a lunch. I sat next to him, and he seemed to me the most nervous human being I've ever seen. He went through absolute hell under Stalin. There were articles about him in the London *Observer*. What this man was subjected to just because he was a composer!

Then I met him again in Philadelphia when they came here. I sometimes spoke to him at the Philadelphia Academy of Music where there are sort of recesses where the walls are thick and the windows are little. We would be there talking, and then he'd be very warm and friendly, and suddenly the head of what they call the Composer's Union would appear in the background and immediately he'd freeze up like that. I felt very badly and awfully touched, because I liked him.

> *Several of your students were at a party of mine recently, and we were talking about your career and how you've had to wait so long to get pieces performed, sometimes a very long time to get a good performance. Joel Feigin brought up a question that I told him I would ask you, although I wouldn't blame you if you didn't want to answer it. You seem very serene about the prospect that eventually your music will be accepted and played well sometime in the future. I was wondering when you acquired this serenity. You made a very definite decision that you wanted to be a composer, but you surely couldn't have known at the age of twelve that you were as great a composer as you have turned out to be.*

I never think of it in those terms. Because, if I may say so, I think that's nonsense. In other words a person who sets out to be a great composer, if that's his aim, either great or not, very likely then he's probably not fit to be a composer at all. I mean, you write music because you love music and you identify with music. You don't think of it in terms of success. With Bloch I came in contact with a man who laughed at the idea of people going in for success. Well, one was in an entirely different world then.

> *I realize that, but I think I'm not expressing the question quite accurately, because I'm not implying that you set*

239

out to be a great composer. I'm just saying that you set out to be a composer and that somewhere along that line between the ages of twelve and eighty-three, either subconsciously or maybe dramatically, you came to the conclusion that you were a great enough composer that your music would survive past your lifetime. And that that may have helped you develop this serenity about which I'm talking.

Well, in the first place one can tell that by just looking around and seeing what goes on in the musical world. Also, if one has lived in the world in a lot of different places and gotten a real sense of what is going on. I had lunch with Joel's father and mother—they're awfully nice people, I'm very fond of them. I was telling them about living in Germany. You get a sense of the larger outlines of what the world is like, of what's going on in it. I'm very depressed about the situation now. I *think* we'll probably come out all right—haven't got much of a choice in the way of presidents [between Carter and Reagan].

That's true.

Awful. Furthermore I know that people do pay attention sometime. Now how long that goes on . . .

I told you about this book of Alfred Einstein's, *Greatness in Music.*[4] He points out that in the first place any legend that any of the great composers was really successful in his lifetime is nonsense. The fact is that Bach was the fourth choice for the job in Leipzig that he got finally. And when he went to see Frederick the Great, he went as an organist, not as a composer at all.

Beethoven was a highly controversial figure during his lifetime. One really knows that Mozart was very discouraged, although he was an infant prodigy and so forth. One realizes how irrelevant . . . and one gets very disillusioned about publicity because the whole thing is so corrupt. You can pay for it. So if there are a few people who really love your music, why, that's the best sign in the world.

I imagine as you say, living in Europe and knowing other people besides musicians . . .

And knowing on the whole the best musicians.

I feel that I know some very good musicians here at Juilliard. When I went to Athens to hear the ISCM World Music Days, I came to the conclusion that American composers not only have equaled European composers but have in general superseded them, although the public does not realize that.

The public is very slow always.

I don't know even whether some of the American composers realize it. Of course, there are some spectacular European composers, individuals. Naturally, there are some spectacular Americans.

There never have been more than a few.

Right. But even the level of the mediocre, I'm saying, is higher in this country now than what I heard at the World Music Days.

However, you know the ISCM never was a . . .

Not representative, you think?

Not wholly.

The level of playing seemed to me a little under the caliber of American performers.

It probably is. It may very well be.

The question came up because of what I call your serenity; it isn't urgent that your music be famous the next day.

My dear Andrea, I'm doing what I want to do. [laughter] That's really what it amounts to.

Sometimes I ask Larry, "Why are you a composer?" And he doesn't know why. He knows that it's not very financially rewarding, and that it's difficult, but he just is one. I said, "I don't know why I'm writing a book on Roger Sessions's music." I mean, no publisher asked me to write a book. Nobody is giving me a degree to write the book, or any money. I just know that I want to write this book and I'm determined to do it, and have done most of it.

I'll tell you one thing. I've talked to one of my students quite a lot. I said to him, "If you live the kind of life I have, you'll never have a lot of money, but you'll have a lot more fun." You see, I've had some wonderful friends. And I learned to talk to very famous people very simply and they liked it. We got along together. I never stood in awe of anybody or anything like that.

> *I think I was before I came to Juilliard, but after being here a couple of years I find people are very approachable. That's why I think you were such a success in my class last Tuesday, because we've been talking about great composers for two years in that course. They're not used to seeing a real live composer in class. They were fascinated with this person who was so approachable and who made them laugh. They adored it. I know they did, because I know them.*

You'd think that Albert Einstein would arouse more apprehension and fear than *anybody,* and yet he was just as simple as he could be. And Stravinsky and Schoenberg (God knows).

> *I think sometimes the pretension of being awesome or standoff-ish is just a purposeful wall to protect famous people from being found out. Maybe they're not as good as everybody thinks they are.*

Yes. It's a kind of insecurity. And also there's something else. I have often been accused, if you want to put it that way, of being very cold and rather haughty. The real truth of the matter is I'm essentially very shy.

I was shy, too, in approaching you *six years ago.*

After all, if somebody goes up to you that you don't know, you feel flattered. [laughter]

When my Eighth Symphony was played in Syracuse, I was addressing a group of students. I was asked whether I would advise a young student of composition to become a composer. I said, "Well, I would answer exactly what I answered a student of mine who asked me whether I'd advise him to get married or not. And I said, 'Since you ask me, no.'" And then my friend Louis Krasner asked me, "When did you decide to become a composer?" I said, "Well, in the fall of 1910 I told my parents I was going to be one." He said, "That's not what I asked you. I asked you when *you* decided." I thought for a few minutes and I said, "But, I never decided. I just knew I was going to be one." He said, "I knew you'd say that." And of course that's really the answer.

NOTES

Introduction

1. Edward T. Cone, "Roger Sessions's *Questions About Music,*" *Perspectives of New Music* (spring-summer 1972), p. 168.
2. Andrea Olmstead, *Roger Sessions and His Music* (Ann Arbor, Mich.: UMI Research Press, 1985).

Orchestral Music

1. Elliott Carter, "Current Chronicle—New York," *Musical Quarterly* 45 (July 1959): 375–81.
2. Andrew Imbrie, "The Symphonies of Roger Sessions," *Tempo* 103 (1972):26.
3. Henry Cowell, "Current Chronicle—New York," *Musical Quarterly* 36 (April 1950): 268–70.
4. Sessions's disregard for the order of pitches in determining row permutations is obvious here. His view of symmetry is practically identical to what has often been called combinatoriality. He seems to prefer a quasi-scalar arrangement of his hexachords in close position, as can be seen in the musical example.

Instrumental Music

1. Roger Sessions, *The Musical Experience of Composer, Performer, Listener* (Princeton, N.J.: Princeton University Press, 1950), pp. 50–53.

245

2. Sessions *did* sometimes fulfill commissions late, but he did not make changes after performances.

3. Jacques Hadamard, *The Psychology of Invention in the Mathematical Field* (Princeton, N.J.: Princeton University Press, 1945), pp. 16–17.

4. Edward T. Cone, "Roger Sessions' String Quartet," *Modern Music* 18 (March 1941): 159–63.

5. Roger Sessions, "Duo for Violin and Piano," liner notes, *Columbia* ML 2169.

6. According to the *New Grove Dictionary of Music and Musicians,* there are only 68 quartets attributable to Haydn.

7. Arnold Schoenberg, *Briefe,* selected and ed. E. Stein (Mainz, 1958; English translation, enlarged, 1964).

Vocal Music

1. Robert Cogan, "Toward a Theory of Timbre: Verbal Timbre and Musical Line in Purcell, Sessions, and Stravinsky," *Perspectives of New Music* 8 (fall 1969): 75–81.

2. Frank Rounds and Edward T. Cone, "The Reminiscences of Roger Sessions," 2 vols., 13 March—24 October 1962 (Columbia University Oral History Collection), p. 316.

Biography

1. Roger Sessions, *Questions about Music* (Cambridge, Mass.: Harvard University Press, 1970).

2. Ruth Huntington Sessions, *Sixty-Odd: A Personal History* (Brattleboro, Vt.: Stephen Daye Press, 1936).

3. James Lincoln Huntington, *Forty Acres: The Story of the Bishop Huntington House* (New York: Hastings House, 1949).

4. Roger Sessions, "The Psychological Basis of Modern Dissonance," *Harvard Musical Review* 3, no. 3 (December 1914): 3–10.

5. Roger Sessions, *Reflections on the Music Life in the United States* (New York: Merlin, 1956).

6. Alfred Einstein, *The Italian Madrigal,* 3 vols., trans. Alexander H. Krappe, Oliver Strunk, and Roger Sessions (Princeton, N.J.: Princeton University Press, 1949).

Analysis and Theory

1. Roger Sessions, *Harmonic Practice* (New York: Harcourt, Brace & World, 1951).
2. Jan La Rue, *Guidelines for Style Analysis* (New York: W. W. Norton, 1970).
3. Edward T. Cone, "Sessions's Concertino," *Tempo* 115 (December 1975): 2–10.

Music and Musicians

1. Barbara W. Tuchman, *A Distant Mirror: The Calamitous 14th Century* (New York: Alfred A. Knopf, 1978).
2. Roger Sessions, program notes for *The Trial of Lucullus,* Juilliard Opera Theater, New York (19 May 1966).
3. Winthrop Sargeant, "Musical Events: Is Music Dead?" *The New Yorker* 44 (11 May 1968): 140.
4. Alfred Einstein, *Greatness in Music,* trans. César Saerchinger (New York: Oxford University Press, 1941; repr. New York: Da Capo, 1971).

LIST OF WORKS AND RECORDINGS

The Black Maskers (1928) (Incidental Music 1923) (for orchestra)
Published by Edward B. Marks, 1960
American Recording Society Orch./Walter Hendl: *Desto* D 404 (mono), DST 6404, DC 6404
Note: Romualdo's Song is not recorded

Eastman-Rochester Sym. Orch./Howard Hanson: *Mercury* MG 50106 (mono), SR 90103, MMA 11145 (mono), AMS 16093, MG 50423 (mono), SR 90423, SRI 75049

Three Chorale Preludes for Organ (1924 and 1926)
Published by Merion Music
Marilyn Mason, organ: *Counterpoint/Esoteric* CTP 522 (mono)

Symphony No. 1 (1927)
Published by Kalmus
Japan Phil. Sym. Orch./Akeo Watanabe: *Composers Recordings Inc.* CRI 131 (mono), CRI SD 131

On the Beach at Fontana (1930)
Published by Edward B. Marks, 1964
Bethany Beardslee, sop.; Robert Helps, piano: *New World Records* NS 243

Note: All recordings are stereo unless otherwise indicated.

Sonata for Piano, No. 1 (1930)
 Published by B. Schotts Söhne, 1931
  Robert Helps: *Composers Recordings Inc.* CRI 198 (mono), CRI
   SD 198
  Rebecca LaBreque: *Opus One* 56/7

Four Pieces for Children (1935–1939) (piano)
 Scherzino and March published by Carl Fischer, 1936; Waltz for
 Brenda and Little Piece published by Edward B. Marks, 1965

Concerto for Violin and Orchestra (1935)
 Published by Edward B. Marks, 1937
  Paul Zukofsky/French Radio and Television Phil. Orch./
   Gunther Schuller: *Composers Recordings Inc.* CRI 220 USD,
   CRI SD 220

String Quartet No. 1 in E Minor (1936)
 Published by Edward B. Marks, 1938
  Pro Arte String Quartet: *New World Records* 302 (mono)
  Galimir Quartet: *Guild Recordings* set no. RSSI (78 r.p.m.)

Chorale for Organ (1938)
 Published by H. W. Gray Co., Inc., 1941

Pages from a Diary (1939) (piano)
 Published by Edward B. Marks, 1947
  Maro Ajemian: *M.G.M.* E 3218 (mono)
  Leon Fleisher: *Epic* LC 3862 (mono); *Columbia* FCX 999
   (mono), SAXF 999
  Herbert Rogers: *Composers Recordings Inc.* CRI SD 281
  Roger Shields: *Vox* set no. SVBX 5303

Duo for Violin and Piano (1942)
 Published by Edward B. Marks, 1966
  Paul Zukofsky, violin; Gilbert Kalish, piano: *Desto* set no. DC
   6435 to DC 6437 (record no. DC 6437)
  Patricia Travers, violin; Otto Herz, piano: *Columbia* set no.
   MM 987

250

Turn, O Libertad (1944) (mixed chorus and piano four-hands)
    Published by Edward B. Marks, 1952
        Gregg Smith Singers/Oresta Cybriwsky and Raymond Beegle,
        piano duet/Gregg Smith: *Vox* set no. SVBX 5353

Symphony No. 2 (1946)
    Published by G. Schirmer, 1949
        Phil. Sym. Orch. of New York/Dimitri Mitropoulos: *Columbia*
        set no. MM 920 (78 r.p.m. records, nos. 13095 D to 13098
        D), ML 2120 (10″ mono), ML 4784 (mono); *Composers Re-*
        cordings Inc. CRI SD 278 (also available on cassette)

Piano Sonata No. 2 (1946)
    Published by Edward B. Marks, 1948
        Randall Hodgkinson: *New World Records* NWR 320
        Rebecca LaBreque: *Opus One* 56/7
        Noël Lee: *Valois* MB 755
        Alan Marks: *Composers Recordings Inc.* S-385
        Beveridge Webster: *Dover* HCR 5265 (mono)

The Trial of Lucullus (1947) (one-act opera in thirteen scenes)

String Quartet No. 2 (1951)
    Published by Edward B. Marks, 1954
        Kohon Quartet: *Vox* set no. SVBX 5305
        New Music Quartet: *Columbia* MS 5105 (mono)

Sonata for Violin Solo (1953)
    Published by Edward B. Marks, 1955
        Hyman Bress: *Folkways* FM 3355 (mono)
        Robert Gross: *Orion* ORS 73110
        Paul Zukofsky: CP^2 1

Idyll of Theocritus (1954) (soprano and orchestra)
    Published by Edward B. Marks, 1957
        Audrey Nossaman, sop./Louisville Orch./Robert Whitney:
        Lou. 57–4 (mono)

Mass for Unison Choir (1955) (male voices)
    Published by Edward B. Marks, 1957

Concerto for Piano and Orchestra (1956)
　Published by Edward B. Marks, 1959

Symphony No. 3 (1957)
　Published by Edward B. Marks, 1962
　　Royal Phil. Orch./Igor Buketoff: *R.C.A.* LSC 3095; *Composers Recordings Inc.* CRI S-451

String Quintet (1958)
　Published by Edward B. Marks, 1959

Symphony No. 4 (1958)
　Published by Edward B. Marks, 1963
　　Columbus Symphony/Christian Badea: *New World Records* NWR 345

Divertimento for Orchestra (1960)
　Published by Theodore Presser, 1982
　　Louisville Orch./Peter Leonard: *Lou.* 776

Montezuma (1963) (opera in three acts)
　Published by Edward B. Marks, 1962

Psalm 140 (1963) (for soprano and organ or orchestra)
　Published by Edward B. Marks, 1964

Symphony No. 5 (1964)
　Published by Edward B. Marks, 1971
　　Columbus Symphony/Christian Badea: *New World Records* NWR 345

Sonata for Piano, No. 3 (1965)
　Published by Edward B. Marks, 1969
　　Robert Helps: *Acoustic Research/Deutsche Grammophon* 0654 086; *New World Records* NRW 307
　　Rebecca LaBreque: *Opus One* 56/7

Symphony No. 6 (1966)
　Published by Theodore Presser, 1975

Six Pieces for Violoncello (1966)
    Published by Edward B. Marks, 1967
      Roy Christensen: *Gasparo* GS 102

Symphony No. 7 (1967)
    Published by Theodore Presser, 1977
      Louisville Orch./Peter Leonard: *Lou.* 776

Symphony No. 8 (1968)
    Published by Edward B. Marks, 1973
      New Philharmonia Orch./Frederik Prausnitz: *Argo* ZRG 702

Rhapsody for Orchestra (1970)
    Published by Theodore Presser, 1981
      New Philharmonia Orch./Frederik Prausnitz: *Argo* ZRG 702
      Columbus Symphony/Christian Badea, *New World Records* NWR 345

When Lilacs Last in the Dooryard Bloom'd (1971) (cantata for soprano, contralto and baritone soloists, mixed chorus, and orchestra)
    Published by Theodore Presser, 1974
      Esther Hinds, sop.; Florence Quivar, mezzo; Dominic Cossa, bar./Tanglewood Festival Chorus, Boston Sym. Orch./Seiji Ozawa: *New World Records* NWR 296

Concerto for Violin, Violoncello, and Orchestra (1971)
    Published by Theodore Presser, 1979

Canons (1971) (for string quartet)
    Published in *Tempo* magazine, 1972

Concertino for Chamber Orchestra (1972)
    Published by Edward B. Marks, 1974
      University of Chicago Chamber Players/Ralph Shapey: *Desto* 7155

Three Choruses on Biblical Texts (1972) (with orchestra)
    Published by Theodore Presser, 1976

Five Pieces for Piano (1975)
>   Published by Theodore Presser, 1976
>>   Robert Black: *Composers Recordings Inc.* CRI S-481

Waltz for Piano (1978)
>   Published by C. F. Peters, 1978
>>   Alan Feinberg: *Nonesuch* 79011 (digital)

Symphony No. 9 (1978)
>   Published by Theodore Presser, 1984

Concerto for Orchestra (1981)
>   Published by Theodore Presser, 1983
>>   Boston Sym. Orch./Seiji Ozawa: *Hyperion* A66050 (digital)

An Introduction to the Works of Rogers Sessions (ninety-minute cassette tape produced by the Kent School, 1987)

BIBLIOGRAPHY

I. Writings by Roger Sessions

"Wagner's Opinions of Other Composers." *Harvard Musical Review* 1, no. 8 (May 1913): 17–20.

"The Case Against Professional Musical Criticism." *Harvard Musical Review* 2, no. 2 (November 1913): 3–6.

"Our Attitude Towards Contemporary Musical Tendencies." *Harvard Musical Review* 2, no. 4 (January 1914): 3–6, 23.

"Book Review of *Symphonies and their Meaning* by Philip H. Goepp." *Harvard Musical Review* 2, no. 5 (February 1914): 22.

"Parsifaliana." *Harvard Musical Review* 2, no. 6 (March 1914): 13–15.

"Fifty Years of Richard Strauss—I." *Harvard Musical Review* 2, no. 8 (May 1914): 12–19.

"Fifty Years of Richard Strauss—II." *Harvard Musical Review* 2, no. 9 (June 1914): 3–12, 18–20.

"Fifty Years of Richard Strauss—III." *Harvard Musical Review* 2, no. 10 (July 1914): 17–25.

"A New Wagner Essay." *Harvard Musical Review* 3, no. 2 (November 1914): 3–7.

"The Psychological Basis of Modern Dissonance." *Harvard Musical Review* 3, no. 3 (December 1914): 3–10.

"Richard Strauss As a Tone Poet." *Harvard Musical Review* 4, no. 1 (October 1915): 4–8.

"Richard Strauss As a Tone Poet—II." *Harvard Musical Review* 4, no. 2 (November 1915): 11–15.

"Richard Strauss As a Tone Poet—III." *Harvard Musical Review* 4, no. 3 (December 1915): 9–13.

"An American Evening Abroad." *Modern Music* 4 (November 1926): 33–36.

*"Ernest Bloch." *Modern Music* 5 (November 1927): 3–11.

*"On *Oedipus Rex.*" *Modern Music* 5 (March 1928): 9–15.

*"Music in Crisis—Some Notes on Recent Musical History." *Modern Music* 10 (January 1933): 63–78.

*"Music and Nationalism; Some Notes on Dr. Göbbel's Letter to Furtwängler." *Modern Music* 11 (November 1933): 3–12.

*"New Vistas in Musical Education." *Modern Music* 11 (March 1934): 115–20.

"Composition and Review." *New York Times* (11 March 1934), p. 10.

Letter on Otto Klemperer's Reading of Beethoven's Fifth Symphony. *New York Times* (28 October 1934), p. 9.

*"Hindemith's *Mathis der Maler.*" *Modern Music* 12 (November 1934): 13–17.

*"Heinrich Schenker's Contribution." *Modern Music* 12 (May 1935): 170–78.

*"America Moves to the Avant-Scene." *American Musicological Society Papers* (1937): 108–19.

*"The New Musical Horizon." *Modern Music* 14 (January 1937): 59–66.

*"Hindemith on Theory." *Modern Music* 15 (November 1937): 57–63.

*"Exposition by Křenek." *Modern Music* 15 (January 1938): 123–28.

*"Escape by Theory." *Modern Music* 15 (March 1938): 192–97.

*"To Revitalize Opera." *Modern Music* 15 (March 1938): 145–52.

*"Vienna—*Vale, Ave.*" *Modern Music* 15 (May 1938): 203–8.

*"The Function of Theory." *Modern Music* 16 (May 1938): 257–68.

*"On the American Future." *Modern Music* 17 (January 1940): 71–75.

*"American Music and the Crisis." *Modern Music* 18 (May 1941): 211–17.

"Musicology and the Composer." *Bulletin of the American Musicological Society* 5 (August 1941): 5–7.

*"The Composer and His Message." In *The Intent of the Artist.* Ed. by Augusto Centano. Princeton, N.J.: Princeton University Press, 1941, pp. 101–34.

*Republished in *Roger Sessions on Music; Collected Essays.*

*"Artists and This War." *Modern Music* 20 (November 1942): 3–7.
*"No More Business-as-Usual." *Modern Music* 19 (March 1942): 156–62.
"How Far Will We Go with Popularization?" *Saturday Review of Literature* 27 (22 January 1944): 25–26.
Letter citing Summer Music Institute, Black Mountain College. *New York Times* (24 September 1944), p. 2.
"Alfred Einstein's Study of Mozart." *New York Times* (18 February 1945), pp. 3, 18, 20.
"Sir Donald Tovey: Musical Articles from the *Encyclopedia Britannica* (and) *Essays in Musical Analysis: Chamber Music.*" *Kenyon Review* (summer 1945): 504–7.
*"Europe Comes to America." 1945.
*"Music in a Business Economy." *Berkeley: A Journal of Modern Culture* (July 1948): 1–2, 7–8.
*"Schönberg in den U.S.A." *Stimmen* 16 (1949): 440–43. Reprinted with revisions in "Schönberg in the United States." *Tempo* 103 (December 1972): 8–17.
Einstein, Alfred. *The Italian Madrigal.* 3 vols., translated by Alexander H. Krappe, Roger H. Sessions, and Oliver Strunk. Princeton, N.J.: Princeton University Press, 1949.
*"The Composer and the University." 1949.
*"How a 'Difficult' Composer Gets That Way." *New York Times* (8 January 1950), p. 2.
The Musical Experience of Composer, Performer, Listener. Princeton, N.J.: Princeton University Press, 1950, and New York: Atheneum, 1962.
Harmonic Practice. New York: Harcourt, Brace & World, 1951.
*"Some Notes on Schönberg and the 'Method of Composing with Twelve Tones.'" *Score* 6 (May 1952): 7–10.
*"Music and the Crisis of the Arts." *Frontiers of Knowledge* (1954): 32–39.
Reflections on the Music Life in the United States. New York: Merlin Press, 1956.
*"Song and Pattern in Music Today." *Score* 17 (September 1956): 73–84.
"Contemporary Music in Our Concert Halls," *Newsletter* of the American Symphony Orchestra League, Charleston, W.V., 8, no. 6 (1957): 15.

*"Thoughts on Stravinsky." *Score* 20 (June 1957): 32–37.

*"Art, Freedom, and the Individual." *Sewanee Review* 66 (1958): 282–96.

"To the Editor." *Score* 23 (July 1958): 58–64.

*"Problems and Issues Facing the Composer Today." *Musical Quarterly* 46 (April 1960): 159–71. Reprinted in *Problems of Modern Music.* Ed. Paul Henry Lang. New York: W. W. Norton, 1962, pp. 21–33.

*"Style and 'Styles' in Music." 1961.

"The Classical Tradition in Music." In *From Sophocles to Picasso,* ed. Whitney J. Oates. Bloomington, Ind.: Indiana University Press, 1962.

"Brickbats and a Bouquet for Sir John." *Musical America* 84 (September 1964): 4.

*"To the Editor." *Perspectives of New Music* 5 (spring-summer 1967): 81–97. Also in *Perspectives on American Composers,* ed. Boretz and Cone. New York: W. W. Norton, 1971, pp. 108–24. Reprinted in *Roger Sessions on Music; Collected Essays,* Princeton, N.J.: Princeton University Press, 1979, under the title "What Can Be Taught?"

Questions About Music. Cambridge, Mass.: Harvard University Press, 1970, and New York: W. W. Norton 1971.

Roger Sessions on Music; Collected Essays. Princeton, N.J.: Princeton University Press, 1979.

II. Writings About Roger Sessions

Abruzzo, James, and Henry Weinberg. "Roger Sessions." In *The New Grove Dictionary of Music and Musicians.* 20 vols., ed. Stanely Sadie. London: Macmillan, 1980. Vol. 17, pp. 194–97.

Austin, William. *Music in the Twentieth Century* New York: W. W. Norton, 1966, pp. 437–39.

Barzun, Jacques. "Not Art for Art's Sake Alone." *Saturday Review of Literature* 34 (28 July 1951): 18–19.

Bauman, Alvin. "Book review of *Harmonic Practice.*" *American Musicological Society Journal* 5 (fall 1952): 265–68.

Berger, Arthur. "Enduring Sessions." *Saturday Review of Literature* 33 (August 1950): 53.

Boretz, Benjamin. "Sessions Festival." *Musical America* 81 (March 1961): 25–26.

———. "Current Chronicle." *Musical Quarterly* 27 (July 1961): 386–96.

Boretz, Benjamin, and Edward T. Cone, eds. *Perspectives on American Composers.* New York: W. W. Norton, 1971.

Broder, Nathan. "Roger Sessions." In *Die Musik in Geschichte und Gegenwart.* 14 vols., ed. Friedrich Blume. Kassel: Bärenreiter. 1965. Vol. 12, cols. 590–91.

Brody, Martin. "Book review." *Journal of Music Theory* 27, no. 1 (spring 1983): 111–20.

Brunswick, Mark. "American Composers, X: Roger Huntington Sessions." *Modern Music* 10 (May 1933): pp. 182–87.

Campbell, Michael Ian. *The Piano Sonatas of Roger Sessions: Sequel to a Tradition.* D.M.A. diss.: Peabody Institute, 1982.

Carter, Elliott. "Spring Fancies, 1937." *Modern Music* 14, no. 4 (May 1937): 216.

———. "The Rhythmic Basis of American Music." *Score* 12 (June 1955): 29.

———. "Current Chronicle—New York." *Musical Quarterly* 45 (July 1959): 375–91.

———. "Roger Sessions: A Commemorative Tribute." *Tempo* 156 (March 1986): 4–6.

Chanler, Theodore. "Current Chronicle." *Musical Quarterly* 44 (April 1958): 228–30.

Chase, Gilbert. *America's Music.* New York: McGraw-Hill, 1955. pp. 525–30.

Cogan, Robert. "Toward a Theory of Timbre: Verbal Timbre and Musical Line in Purcell, Sessions, and Stravinsky." *Perspectives of New Music* 8 (fall 1969): 75–81.

Cone, Edward T. "Sessions: Second String Quartet." *Musical Quarterly* 43 (January 1957): 140–41.

———. "Analysis Today." *Musical Quarterly* (April 1960): 172–88.

———. "Conversations with Roger Sessions." *Perspectives of New Music* 4 (spring 1966): 29–46. Reprinted in Boretz and Cone, *Perspectives on American Composers,* pp. 90–107.

———. "Book review of *Questions About Music.*" *Perspectives of New Music* 10 (spring-summer 1972): 164–70.

————. "In Honor of Roger Sessions." *Perspectives of New Music* 10 (spring-summer 1972): 130–41.

————. "In Defense of Song: The Contribution of Roger Sessions." *Critical Inquiry* 2, no. 1 (autumn 1975): 93–112.

————. "Sessions's Concertino." *Tempo* 115 (December 1975): 2–10.

————. "A Tribute To Roger Sessions," *Kent Quarterly* 5, no. 2 (winter 1986): 29–31.

Copland, Aaron. "America's Young Men of Promise." *Modern Music* 3 (March 1926): 13–20.

————. "Contemporaries at Oxford, 1931." *Modern Music* 9 (November 1931): 22–23.

————. "The American Composer Gets a Break." *American Mercury* 34 (April 1935): 490–91.

————. "Sessions and Piston," *Our New Music.* New York: Mc-Graw-Hill, 1941, pp. 176–86. Revised and enlarged in *The New Music 1900–1960.* New York: W. W. Norton, 1968, pp. 127–34.

Copland, Aaron, and Vivian Perlis. *Copland/1900–1942.* New York: St. Martin's/Marek, 1984.

Cowell, Henry. "Current Chronicle: New York." *Musical Quarterly* 36 (January 1950): 94–98.

————. "Current Chronicle: New York." *Musical Quarterly* 36 (April 1950): 268–70.

Danchenka, Gary Robert. *Quantitative Measurement of Information Content via Recurring Associations* in *Three Movements of Symphony No. 2 by Roger Sessions.* Ph.D. diss.: University of Miami, 1981.

————. "A new way of measuring musical affect," *Indiana Theory Review* 5, no. 2 (1982): 34–61.

Daniel, Oliver. "Roger Sessions." *Ovation* (March 1984): 12–15, 48.

Diamond, David. "Roger Sessions: Symphony No. 2." *Notes* 7 (June 1950): 438–39.

Duffin, Diana Ruth. *The Interpretation of Accent Signs in Roger Sessions's Third Piano Sonata.* D.M.A. diss.: Ohio State University, 1979.

Epstein, D. M. "Sessions at 60—An Appraisal of His Work." *Musical America* 77 (September 1957): 28.

Ewen, David. *Composers Since 1900.* New York: H. W. Wilson, 1969, pp. 519–22.

Ferro, E. F. "Los Conciertos." *Buenos Aires Musical* 20, no. 331 (1965): 2–3.

Foldes, Andor. "Roger Sessions: Second Sonata for Piano Solo." *Notes* 7 (March 1950): 312–13.

Gagne, Cole, and Tracy Caras. "Roger Sessions." In *Sound-Pieces: Interviews with American Composers.* Metuchen, N.J.: Scarecrow Press, 1982, pp. 355–65.

Goldman, Richard F. "Current Chronicle." *Musical Quarterly* 46 (January 1960): 71–73.

Greissle, Felix, and Lester Trimble. "Current Chronicle." *Musical Quarterly* 43 (April 1957): 236–40.

Harbison, John. "Roger Sessions and Montezuma." *New Boston Review* (June 1976). Reprinted in *Tempo* 121 (June 1977): 2–5.

Harbison, John, and Andrea Olmstead. "Roger Sessions." In *The New Grove Dictionary of American Music.* Ed. H. Wiley Hitchcock. New York: Macmillan, 1986, 4:192–97.

Henahan, Donal. "Roger Sessions." *New York Times* (14 April 1968), p. 2.

———. Obituary. *New York Times* (18 March 1985), p. B6.

Henderson, Ronald D. *Tonality in the Pre-Serial Instrumental Music of Roger Sessions.* Ph.D. diss.: Eastman School of Music, 1974.

Hitchcock, H. Wiley. "Current Chronicle." *Musical Quarterly* 50 (July 1964): 381–82.

Howard, John Tasker. *Our Contemporary Composers.* New York: Thomas Y. Crowell, 1941.

———. *Our American Music.* 4th ed. New York: Thomas Y. Crowell, 1965.

Howard, John Tasker, and George Kent Bellows. *A Short History of Music in America.* New York: Thomas Y. Crowell, 1957, pp. 293–95.

Imbrie, Andrew. "Current Chronicle." *Musical Quarterly* 44 (July 1958): 370–71.

———. "Roger Sessions: In Honor of His 65th Birthday." *Perspectives of New Music* 1 (fall 1962): 117–47. Reprinted in Boretz and Cone, *Perspectives on American Composers,* pp. 59–89.

———. "The Symphonies of Roger Sessions." *Tempo* 103 (1972): 24–32.

———. "Remembering Roger And His Second Symphony," *Kent Quarterly* 5, no. 2 (winter 1986): 11–16.

Kastendieck, M. "Roger Sessions." *Broadcast Music Incorporated* (February 1968): 9.

Keats, Sheila. "Reference Articles on American Composers: An Index." *Juilliard Review* 1 (fall 1954): 32–33.

Kress, Steven Morton. *Roger Sessions, Composer and Teacher: a Comparative Analysis of Roger Sessions' Philosophy of Educating Composers and his Approach to Composition in Symphonies no. 2 and 8.* Ph.D. diss.: University of Florida, 1982.

Laufer, Edward C. "Roger Sessions: *Montezuma.*" *Perspectives of New Music* 4 (fall 1965): 95–108.

Machlis, Joseph. *Introduction to Contemporary Music,* 2d ed. New York: W. W. Norton, 1979, pp. 398–407.

Mason, Charles Norman. *A Comprehensive Analysis of Roger Sessions's Opera "Montezuma."* D.M.A. diss.: University of Illinois, Urbana-Champaign, 1982.

Merryman, Marjorie Jane. *Aspects of phrasing and pitch usage in Roger Sessions's Piano Sonata No. 3.* Ph.D. diss.: Brandeis University, 1981.

Mishin, Henry G. "The Genesis of a Commission: Roger Sessions, Three Choruses on Biblical Texts." Published by The Friends of Amherst College Music on the occasion of the Amherst College Sesquicentennial Celebration, n.d.

"Moments Musicaux. Roger Sessions: Celebration of his 80 Years." *Perspectives of New Music* 16, no. 1 (1978): 85–154 (music by Imbrie, Helps, Lansky, Diamond, Gamer, Babbitt, Randall, Gideon, Kirchner, Cone, Boretz, Fine, Swift, Lewin, Westergaard, Weisgall, Spies).

Neuman, K. "6 Pieces for Violoncello." *Notes* 25, no. 3 (March 1969): 599–600.

Oja, Carol. "The Copland–Sessions Concerts." *Musical Quarterly* 65 (April 1979): 212–29.

Olmstead, Andrea. "Roger Sessions: A Personal Portrait." *Tempo* 127 (December 1978): 10–16.

———. "Roger Sessions's Ninth Symphony." *Tempo* 133 (December 1980): 79–81.

———. "Roger Sessions On Music; Collected Essays." *Perspectives of New Music* (spring-fall 1981): 491–500.

———. "The Plum'd Serpent: Antonio Borgese's and Roger Sessions's *Montezuma.*" *Tempo* 152 (March 1985): 13–22.

—————. *Roger Sessions and His Music*. Ann Arbor, Mich.: UMI Research Press, 1985.

—————. "Roger Sessions and Twentieth-Century Music," *Kent Quarterly* 5, no. 2 (winter 1986): 6–10.

—————. *An Introduction to the Works of Roger Sessions*. Ninety-minute cassette tape produced by the Kent School, 1987.

Petrobelli, Pierluigi, and Henry Weinberg. "Roger Sessions e la musica americana." *Nuova Rivista Musicale Italiana* 5 (March-April 1971): 249–63.

Pinchman, Tracy. "Sessions' Vocal Music." *Kent Quarterly* 5, no. 2 (winter 1986): 17–20.

Piston, Walter. "Book review of *Harmonic Practice."* *Musical Quarterly* 38 (July 1952): 457–68.

Porter, Andrew. "The Matter of Mexico." *The New Yorker* (19 April 1976): 115–20.

—————. "An American Requiem." *The New Yorker* (April 1977): 133–40.

—————. "Sessions' Passionate and Profound *Lilacs."* *High Fidelity* (February 1978): pp. 70–71.

—————. "Celebration." *The New Yorker* (9 November 1981): 164–67.

—————. "A Magnificent Epic." *The New Yorker* (March 1982): 128–37.

—————. "Musical Events." *The New Yorker* 58 (31 January 1983): 94ff.

Rapoport, Paul. "Roger Sessions: a Discography," *Tempo* 127 (December 1978): 17–20.

Rockwell, John. "Roger Sessions, Nearing 85, Is Still a Maverick Composer." *New York Times* (22 March 1981), pp. 17–18.

"Roger Sessions." Pamphlet. New York: Broadcast Music, Inc., 1965.

Romano, J. "Musicos de hoy: Roger Sessions." *Buenos Aires Musical* 20, no. 332 (1965): 5–6.

—————. "Retratos de musicos americanos: Roger Sessions." *Buenos Aires Musical* 24, no. 400 (1969): 3.

Rosenfeld, Paul. "Roger Sessions." In *Port of New York*. New York: Harcourt & Brace, 1924, pp. 145–52.

—————. "The Newest American Composers." *Modern Music* 15 (March-April 1938): 153–59.

Salzman, Eric. "An American International." *New York Times Book Review* (18 March 1979), p. 9.

Schubart, Mark A. "Roger Sessions: Portrait of an American Composer." *Musical Quarterly* 32 (April 1946): 196–214.

Schweitzer, Eugene. *Generation in String Quartets of Carter, Sessions, Kirchner, and Schuller.* Ph.D. diss.: Eastman School of Music, 1965.

Sessions, Ruth Huntington. *Sixty-Odd; a Personal History.* Brattleboro, Vt.: Stephen Daye Press, 1936.

Sirota, Victoria. "The Keyboard Works of Roger Sessions," *Kent Quarterly* 5, no. 2 (winter 1986): 21–28.

Slonimsky, Nicolas. "Composers of New England." *Modern Music* 7 (February 1930): 24–27.

————. "Roger Sessions." In *American Composers on American Music.* Ed. Henry Cowell. Palo Alto, Cal.: Stanford University Press, 1933, pp. 75–81.

————. "The Six of American Music." *Christian Science Monitor Weekly Magazine* (17 March 1937), pp. 8–9.

————. *Music Since 1900.* New York: Charles Scribner's Sons, 1971.

Tischler, Hans. *Notes* 9 (June 1952): 409–10.

Vinton, John, ed. "Roger Sessions." In *Dictionary of Contemporary Music.* New York: E. P. Dutton, 1974, p. 675.

Welch, Roy D. "A Symphony Introduces Roger Sessions." *Modern Music* 4 (May 1927), pp. 27–30.

Wheeler, Scott. *Sessions's Quintet, first movement.* Ph.D. diss.: Brandeis University, 1984.

Whittall, Arnold. "Book reviews." *Music Review* 43, no. 1 (1982): 68–72.

Wright, Lesley. "Roger Huntington Sessions: a Selective Bibliography and a Listing of his Compositions." *Current Musicology* 15 (1973): 107–25.

INDEX

Accent, 55, 75, 187–88, 204, 205, 231; compared with syncopation, 22; in Italian language, 218; on the organ, 143

Accentuation, 75

Acoustics, 123, 157, 196

Aeschylus, 121

Alexander the Great, 238

Alto clarinet, 27

Alto flute, 16, 28

America, music in, 235; musical life in, 26

Americanism in music, 216–17

Analysis, 192–93, 211

Analysts, 209

Ansermet, Ernest, 21–22, 220, 221

Aspen Music Festival, 1

Associative elements, 78–79, 190

Atonality, 56, 73

"Austrian sixth," 197

Aztecs, 134

Bach, Johann Sebastian, 5, 20, 26, 73, 194, 201, 218, 240;

B-minor Mass, 127; chorale, 169; fugue, 87; *Kunst der Fuge,* 87; sonatas, 84

Bach, Philipp Emanuel, 235

Bar lines, 95

Barati, George, 231

Bassett horn, 27–28

Beethoven, Ludwig van, 68, 72, 128, 150, 210, 235, 241; as a pianist, 100; Bagatelles (op. 126), 231; cello sonatas (op. 102), 231; Diabelli Variations, 39; *Fidelio,* 228; *Hammerklavier* Sonata (op. 106), 87, 99–100; *Missa Solemnis,* 127; performance of quartets, 233; piano writing, 99–100; Quartet (op. 18 no. 1), 187; Quartet in C-sharp minor (op. 131), 79, 87, 210; Quartet (op. 132), 62, 88; Sonata for Piano (op. 111), 99–100; symphonies, 73; Symphony No. 3 (*Eroica*), 19, 39, 60–61, 210; Symphony No. 4, 109; Symphony No. 6 (*Pastorale*), 19, 109; Sym-

265